A Traveller's Guide to

ROMAN
BRITAIN

A Traveller's Guide to
ROMAN BRITAIN

Patrick Ottaway & Michael Cyprien

ROUTLEDGE & KEGAN PAUL
London, Boston, Melbourne and Henley

CONTENTS

Introduction 5

Roman Sites in Britain 9

*National map showing the location
of sites described in the gazetteer*

Roman Britain 10–124

*A gazetteer to the sites
including the special articles listed below*

Glossary of Characters 125

Glossary of Terms 126

Further Reading 128

First published in 1987 by Historical Times Incorporated,
2245 Kohn Road, Harrisburg, PA 17105, USA
and by Routledge & Kegan Paul plc
11 New Fetter Lane, London EC4P 4EE and
29 West 35th Street, New York, NY 10001, USA

Text by Patrick Ottaway
Photography and Art Direction by Michael Cyprien
Copy Editor Carole Fries
Filmset in England by BAS Printers Limited,
Over Wallop, Stockbridge, Hampshire
Printed in England by Balding + Mansell Limited
Wisbech, Cambridgeshire

Library of Congress Cataloging in Publication Data
Ottaway, Patrick.
  A traveller's guide to Roman Britain.

  Bibliography: p.
  1. Romans—Great Britain—Antiquities—Guide-books.
  2. Great Britain—Antiquities, Roman—Guide-books.
  3. Historic sites—Great Britain—Guide-books.
  4. Great Britain—Description and travel—1971—
  —Guide-books. I. Cyprien,   Michael. II. Title.
DA145.087   1986   914.1′04858   86–19448
ISBN 0–918678–19–6

British Library Cataloguing in Publication Data also available

ISBN 0 7102 0943 6

INTRODUCTION

A.D. 43 is one of those crucial dates in British history, like 1066, because it was in that year that the Roman Emperor Claudius sent his general, Aulus Plautius, with 40,000 men to conquer this country. In the ensuing forty years or so, a substantial part of Britain was to become a province of the greatest empire the world has ever known, and it remained so for over 300 years – by turns peaceful and turbulent, but always a fascinating period.

Anyone who has visited places such as Bath, with its great temple and bathing establishment, Wroxeter where the battered and enigmatic 'Old Work' still stands, or Housesteads, a fort set high on the Northumbrian crags, must surely feel a compelling desire to know more of what these remains mean, how they come to be there and who built them. The ghosts of proud soldiers, busy townsmen, fashionable women, ambitious freed slaves and all the other sorts and conditions of humanity who populated Roman Britain seem to lurk behind every stretch of ancient masonry or beyond every grassy ditch and rampart, calling to us over the centuries. Indeed, in York there are still local inhabitants who have no doubts that spectral Roman soldiers can still be seen marching towards the legionary headquarters beneath the great medieval Minster. Whether you are in the heart of one of Britain's historic cities, however, or deep in the countryside at the deserted town of Caistor St Edmund, or at Rockbourne villa, you will often find it is the evocative ambience of the Roman sites, rather than simply the remains themselves, which will first strike you. Try to understand them, therefore, in relation to the landscape. Thus look at the lie of the land, as well as the earthworks or wall footings, and ask yourself such questions as: Why did they settle in just this spot? How could it be defended? Where did the water come from? What caused it to grow or decline? Tune in to what the Romans themselves called the *genius loci*, or spirit of place.

Although buildings and other structural remains are often elusive, we know that the Roman genius for architecture and engineering was exercised in Britain, as a trip along Hadrian's Wall or to the Caerleon amphitheatre will immediately prove. One reason why we have little to compare with the great sites of North Africa or Asia Minor, however, is that in Britain, which had a plentiful supply of timber, many buildings were made of wood and they have, of course, long since disappeared. Masonry has also gone because Roman buildings have proved to be convenient quarries in a country where good construction material has always been at a considerable premium, and you will often see Roman brick or stone reused in later buildings such as, for example, the Anglo-Saxon churches at Corbridge or St Martin's, Canterbury.

Roman structures which have survived on anything like a substantial scale are primarily defensive works which were recommissioned in both Anglo-Saxon and medieval times. This explains the fine preservation of upstanding stretches of fortress wall at Chester and York, and of town walls such as those at Caerwent and Colchester. It is not only the later reuse of defences, however, which gives this country so much to offer the student of Roman fortifications. Since the majority of forts were erected in the north and west of Britain, where the conquest was more strenuously resisted but where subsequent development has been less intense, some of our military earthworks have remained largely untouched since Roman times. In their way, fort sites such as Ardoch and Whitley Castle, with their multiple defensive ditches, are among the most spectacular sites of Roman Britain, if not the Roman Empire.

In the more Romanized south and east of England, the focus of attention inevitably moves from military to civilian sites. Many modern towns and cities have grown up on sites originally selected in the first or second centuries A.D. and, in addition to the continuing influence of the Roman defences on the town plan, the streets themselves, of places such as Chichester or Gloucester, may be on or close to the original Roman line. Although few town buildings still survive, the prosperity and diversity of the town life of the period can be readily appreciated in museum displays such as those at Cirencester, York and the Museum of London.

Around the towns, and dependent on them for the sale of their produce, lay the villas which may have been somewhat humble versions of the great country retreats of the upper classes in Italy, but still had a style that was quintessentially Roman. Again, you may find little surviving above ground, although what remains below ground may be spectacular, as at Lullingstone with its underground shrine, but you will still find it of considerable interest to see how a villa plan has developed, perhaps from one of a few small rooms to one with large complex wings ranged around a great courtyard. Look around the countryside, too, and try to assess the natural advantages of the site, often still evident in the present landscape in spite of modern farming developments. The principal attractions of most villa sites today, however, are the mosaic pavements, many of which rank among the great artistic achievements of the period with their complex geometric patterns or scenes depicting natural phenomena or classical mythology.

Taken as a whole, the remains of Roman Britain are something of a patchwork and their enjoyment and appreciation must often be a subtle process requiring both a little imagination and a certain amount of background knowledge. Travellers will soon become aware, however, that we are fortunate in this country in having a great tradition of antiquarian and archaeological scholarship. Since at least the seventeenth century, countless enthusiasts – usually diligent, sometimes daft, occasionally both – have worked tirelessly, examining finds, plotting sites and digging holes. Amongst them we should perhaps mention William Stukeley who, as one of his many projects, drew the earliest map of Roman London in 1722 and then, along with his Society of Roman Knights, gave the Druids a place in the popular imagination which they have never lost. For the beginnings of systematic archaeological investigation, however, we must go forward some 150 years to General Pitt-Rivers, the first Inspector of Ancient Monuments, whose methods of recording – which he developed on excavations of pre-historic and Roman sites on his Cranborne Chase estate in Wiltshire – set new standards not equalled during his lifetime. Thirdly, no history of Romano-British archaeology is complete without Sir Mortimer Wheeler who, during the 1920s and 1930s, was almost singlehandedly responsible for developing techniques of modern fieldwork which are used all over the world. He took as his laboratory a number of important Roman sites, including St Albans and Brecon Gaer, where he not only unravelled the details of their own history, but set the whole study of Roman Britain on a new footing for the scholars who have inherited his mantle.

Since Wheeler's time there has been a great increase in the systematic and detailed excavation of Romano-British sites, often in advance of redevelopment in historic towns, or mining and agricultural operations in rural areas. Alongside this 'rescue archaeology', there have been new discoveries in the scientific examination of artefacts which can tell us when, how and where they were made. We also have new techniques of prospecting, including aerial photography which can spot buried sites where no trace is perceptible on the ground. Another exciting development is the life-size reconstruction which can both inform the visitor and reveal the practicalities of building – for example, a turf and timber rampart or a piece of Hadrian's Wall – in a way that theoretical speculation can never do. One of the first Roman buildings to be reconstructed was the fort at Cardiff Castle, but travellers will also be thrilled by examples at Baginton, Chesterholm, Manchester and, soon, South Shields. Finally, there are the dedicated societies and individuals who re-enact the less tangible aspects of Roman life, among whom the legionaries of the Ermine Street Guard are justly the most famous.

Although archaeology and its offshoots are so important for our understanding of Roman Britain, we must not forget that there are also written sources. When Britain became part of the Roman Empire, it at last moved into the historical record, and there are numerous references to this country in the works of Roman authors. It is necessary to be careful, however, in our interpretation of them since they were not usually intended to provide a purely factual description of people or events. Few of the authors, moreover, wrote from a direct knowledge of Britain, although Tacitus, for one, certainly had first-hand information from his father-in-law, the governor Agricola. The usual intention was rather to entertain the reader with the curiosities, however far-fetched, of distant lands, or to present them with moral lessons applicable to the politics of Rome itself. When Cassius Dio, for example, describes Britain north of Hadrian's Wall by saying, 'They dwell in tents, naked and unshod, possess their women in common and in common rear all their offspring', he is clearly employing an element of artistic licence. Similarly, when Tacitus has the British leader, Caratacus, taken to Rome as a prisoner, utter such portentous lines as 'If you want to rule the world does it follow that everyone else welcomes enslavement?', he is surely not quoting verbatim.

Another category of written evidence is inscriptions. Fortunately for us, the Romans had a tradition of carving in stone, and travellers will soon become familiar with tombstones, milestones and commemorations of public works and religious duties. They are especially common in places which had highly Romanized populations of soldiers and government officials, such as London, Lincoln, York, or the forts along Hadrian's Wall. For day-to-day correspondence and records, people wrote on wooden writing tablets and one of the most fascinating new written sources for Roman Britain to emerge in recent years are those from Chesterholm, near Hadrian's Wall, which record the daily business of a working fort around the year A.D. 100. Finally, we should not forget the curses written on lead plates from the sacred spring at Bath and other religious sites, and the even less formal 'graffiti' – words or phrases scratched on a variety of humble objects such as tiles or potsherds.

Perhaps the most striking impression one is left with after surveying the evidence, both archaeological and written, is of the thoroughness with which a sizeable part of a relatively backward and remote island was integrated into an empire which was sophisticated in an economic, political and cultural sense, and covered not only half of Europe but also much of North Africa and the Near East. Integration is really the key word here, since it is important to appreciate that the Roman Empire cannot really be compared with European colonial empires because there was no lasting attempt to maintain a permanent distinction between the conquerors and conquered. Instead, a uniquely cosmopolitan atmosphere prevailed with little of the racist and nationalist attitudes which plague the modern world. Emperors might come from Italy, Spain, Syria, Africa, or Gaul and government officials and soldiers could expect to serve in a very wide variety of places during their careers. We also know that merchants – like Barathes buried at Corbridge but originally from Palmyra, or Philo buried at Cirencester but originally from south-east Gaul – travelled widely, spreading cultural and religious ideas as well as their goods.

Having said this, we must remember that in the early years of the conquest of Britain there was certainly a sharp division between the Roman and the native. The first frontier zone of the province – which by about A.D. 47 ran along the Fosse Way between, perhaps, Gloucester and Lincoln – was reached after some hard fighting, although some Britons welcomed the Romans for political reasons of their own. Further heavy fighting ensued when the army moved out into the mountains of Wales or north into Brigantia and the revolt of Boudicca in A.D. 60–1 shows that the loss of freedom was not accepted without considerable reluctance in some areas.

By the reign of Hadrian, however, when the northern frontier had been secured along the great Wall which now bears his name, the province was largely at peace and the only subsequent fighting in the island during the Roman era was almost exclusively against external enemies. From having been despised barbarians, the Britons were now able to take some pride in their progress towards civilization Roman-style, and probably looked down, in their turn, on barbarians in the far north or across the Irish Sea. The British woman, Claudia Rufima, known to the poet Martial, probably took as a compliment his lines:

Though brought up among the sky-blue Britons
She has the spirit of the latin race

in spite of his tactless reference to woad.

Although barbarians outside the empire were to remain, in varying degrees, a constant menace to its security, there appears to have been no serious problem in Britain until after the middle of the fourth century A.D. In A.D. 367, either by some unlucky chance or as a result of the plans of some unusually clever leader, all the barbarians menacing Rome's British provinces, whether from Scotland, Ireland or across the North Sea, managed to unite in an attack which caused havoc.

One answer to such incursions, which was adopted increasingly by the imperial government in the later fourth century A.D., was on the 'set a thief to catch a thief' principle, and involved the recruitment of large numbers of Germanic people from outside the empire into the army. Some of these men rose to very high office in Rome, but an overreliance on mercenaries was ultimately a source of weakness, and it was the Anglo-Saxons from northern Germany who were to inherit the rich farmlands of south and east England which had once been coveted by the Romans themselves, leaving the Britons to gradually withdraw into the 'Celtic Fringe' of the north and west.

It is customary to date the end of Roman Britain to A.D. 410, the year of the so-called 'rescript of Honorius' – a letter from the emperor to the cities of Britain telling them to look to their own defence, perhaps in response to some appeal following the failure of the last British-based claimant to the imperial throne, Constantine III. It should be stressed, however, that there can be no suggestion of a sudden or apocalyptic change in the condition of Britain at this time. The popular image of the legions packing their bags and leaving is quite wrong and quite probably owes a good deal to the experience of modern European armies departing from their overseas colonies. It is nearer the truth to conclude that Britain attempted to remain an integral and functioning part of the Roman Empire until at least A.D. 410 and, in spite of being short of regular troops, was still able to defend itself reasonably successfully until the mid-fifth century A.D., or even later. The few English rulers we know of in the fifth or early sixth centuries A.D. certainly seem to have attempted to rule in the Roman style; indeed King Arthur, for whom there is still no really good historical or archaeological evidence, has, nevertheless, been referred to by some scholars as the last British emperor.

The transition from Roman Britain to medieval Britain may be seen, therefore, as a continuously unfolding tapestry with few completely severed threads. Although, as A. E. Houseman wrote of Wroxeter in his famous poem 'A Shropshire Lad',

Today the Roman and his trouble
are ashes under Uricon

the Romans are no less our ancestors than any of the other people who have lived, loved, worked, fought and died in the British Isles.

Access to Sites
Access to most of the sites in the guide is usually possible at any reasonable time. Others, especially the villas, have more restricted opening hours which often
vary according to the season. The principal authorities
responsible for Roman sites in Britain are:

English Heritage
Fortress House
23 Saville Row
LONDON W1X 2HE

CADW
Brunel House
2 Fitzalan Road
Cardiff CF2 1UY

Historic Buildings and Monuments
Scottish Development Department
3–11 Melville Street
Edinburgh EH3 7QD

The National Trust
36 Queen Annes Gate
LONDON SW1H 9AS

They will provide further information on request.
Museums containing Roman antiquities are usually
open daily.
   Travellers are recommended to use the Ordnance
Survey 1:50,000 Landranger Series maps when visiting sites and a six-figure grid reference is given next
to each entry in the guide. Please remember to respect
farmers' property and livestock when looking for sites
in rural areas and, where possible, ask permission
from the landowner.

Front cover, Richborough,
back cover and frontispiece, mosaics at Littlecote

ROMAN SITES IN BRITAIN

This numbered list keys the featured sites to the accompanying map of Great Britain

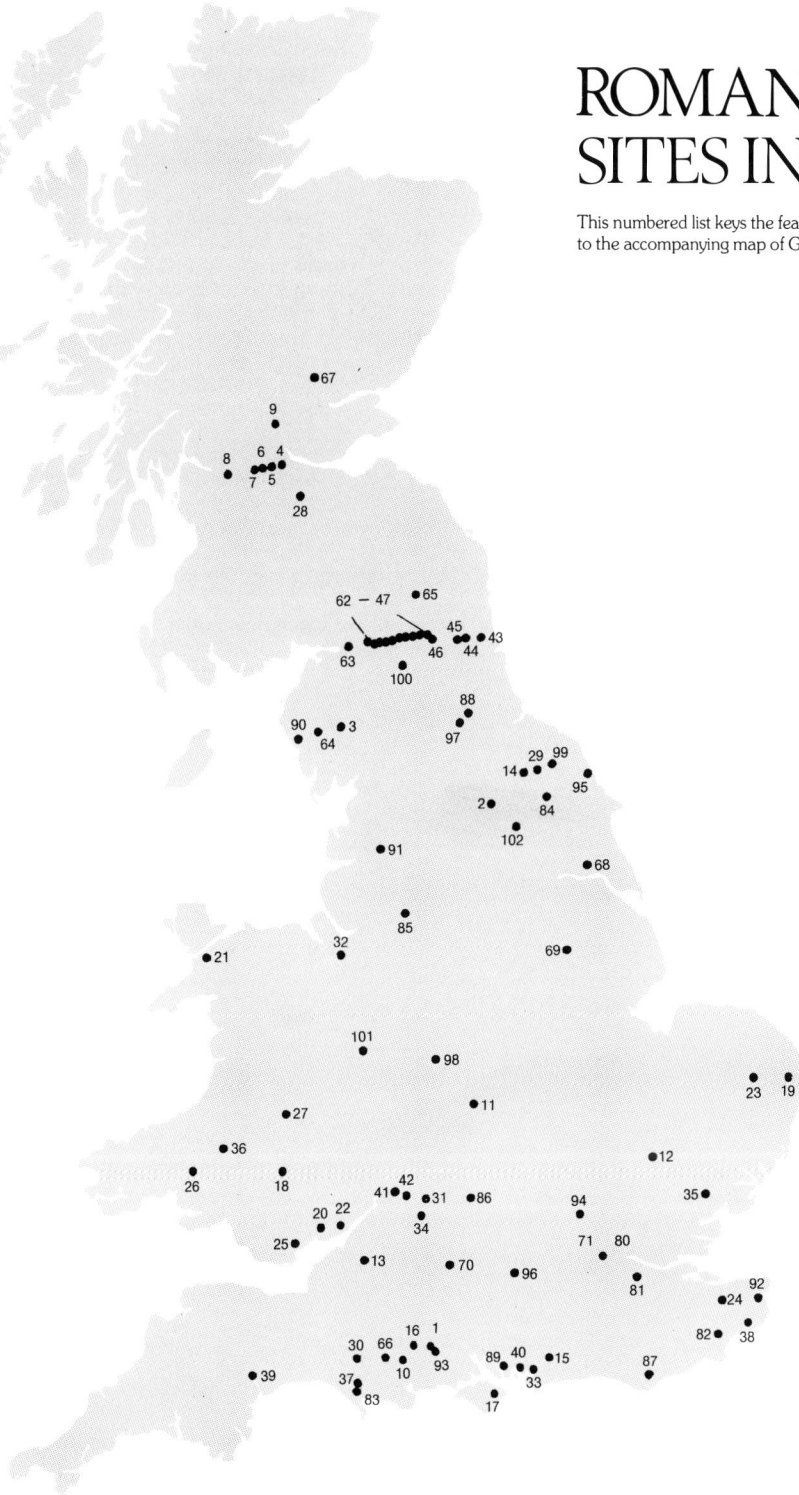

62 Banks East
63 Carlisle
64 Hardknott
65 High Rochester
66 Hod Hill
67 Inchtuthil
68 Kingston upon Hull
69 Lincoln
70 Littlecote
London
71   Noble Street
72   Bastion House
73   St Alphege's
74   Dukes Place
75   Cooper's Row
76   Tower Hill
77   Tower of London
78   Temple of Mithras
79   Museum of London
80   British Museum
81 Lullingstone
82 Lympne
83 Maiden Castle
84 Malton
85 Manchester
86 North Leigh
87 Pevensey
88 Piercebridge
89 Portchester
90 Ravenglass
91 Ribchester
92 Richborough
93 Rockbourne
94 St Albans
95 Scarborough
96 Silchester
97 Stanwick
98 Wall
99 Wheeldale
100 Whitley Castle
101 Wroxeter
102 York

ACKLING DYKE
Dorset
OS 184 SU015163
The Roman road can be found on the left-hand side of the A354 about 14 miles south-west of Salisbury.

One of the most prominent stretches of Roman road in Britain runs north-east to south-west near the Hampshire–Dorset border, south of Salisbury. Originally, the road, now known as the Ackling Dyke, ran from Old Sarum (Sorviodunum), a little to the north of modern Salisbury, to Badbury Rings. What you see is the platform, or *agger*, on which the road itself was constructed. Enthusiastic travellers will be able to follow the dyke for several miles south-east of the point where it meets the modern A354.
See **Badbury Rings, Bokerley Dyke, Roads.**

ALDBOROUGH
(Isurium Brigantum)
North Yorkshire
OS 99 SE 405665
Aldborough is a little to the south-east of the small town of Boroughbridge, which is about 1 mile off the A1. It can also be reached via the A59 and B6265 from York which is 22 miles away.

Roman Britain experienced a great wave of town foundation in the late first century A.D. In the more remote areas of Wales and the north, however, there was little urbanization until the reign of Hadrian (A.D. 117–38), and these later towns, such as Aldborough, Caerwent and Carmarthen, found it difficult to gather momentum for sustained growth. Perhaps this was for economic reasons, perhaps because they were unwilling to adopt a Roman culture in which town life was regarded as the height of civilization.

Expectations of growth at Aldborough seem to have been high for a time, since the circuit of defences established in the late second century A.D. enclosed 55 acres, but the *civitas* capital of the Brigantes never seems to have used all this space. The native population either preferred to remain countrymen or, if they were attracted by urban living, they may have gone to York instead.

Relatively little controlled excavation has been undertaken within the town, but a few mosaics have been found and two second-century A.D. examples can be seen *in situ*. One is perfectly preserved and has a geometric design with an eight-pointed star at its centre; the other had a lion lying beneath a tree at the centre, but this scene is now incomplete. A third mosaic is to be seen in Leeds Museum: this depicts the wolf which suckled the legendary founders of Rome, Romulus and his twin brother Remus. The craftsmanship is crude but the pavement shows that one of the empire's most potent myths was familiar even in its remoter parts.

The other Roman remains to be seen at Aldborough are in a pleasant park near the museum on the south side of the town where the lower courses of the third-century A.D. defensive wall can be seen. The plinth still survives in places. The stone is a local sandstone, but it is known that the town gates were built of millstone grit – a stone also favoured by the Romans in York for sculpture and monumental architecture.

In the small museum there are a number of finds from the site but look out, in particular, for two milestones dating from the reign of the Emperor Decius (249–51) and a somewhat damaged relief of the god Mercury. This may be compared with another Roman relief in the Parish church which may be Mercury or perhaps some local horned-headed deity.
See **York, Towns.**

AMBLESIDE (Galava)
Cumbria
OS 90 NY 372034
Ambleside can be reached from the M6 by taking the Kendal exit 22 miles to the south-east. The fort lies on the south side of the town. Follow the one-way street system onto the A591 Windermere road, and at the road junction by Lake Windermere turn right. The site is a short way along on the left.

Shallow footings at Ambleside.

The setting of Ambleside Fort is one of the most dramatic in Britain; it has Lake Windermere on its south side and the magnificent Cumbrian Fells beyond it to the north. This location was, however, determined by strategic considerations and not by the Roman army's appreciation of a beauty spot. The fort was probably founded as part of the famous Governor Agricola's occupation of the Lake Counties in the early 80s; it guards the east end of a road reaching to Ravenglass on the coast and the heads of two valleys from which the rivers Brathay and Rothay run into the lake.

Nothing survives of the earliest fort; the visible remains are of an early-second-century A.D. stone fort constructed when Roman possession of the area was seen as permanent. On the line of the defences, you can see the base of the main east and south gates. Inside the fort, there are the footings of the commander's house in its usual place next to the *principia*. You should note the underground strong room in the rear range of rooms, where the garrison pay chests were stored.
See **Hardknott, Ravenglass, The Army.**

10

The Wall at Falkirk.

The construction of Hadrian's Wall was only just complete when the order came from Rome to move the northern frontier some 100 miles further north to a line between the Forth and the Clyde.

The only literary reference to this event comes from the biography of the Emperor Antoninus Pius and reads as follows: "Through his legates he carried on many wars, for he subdued the Britons through Lollius Urbicus, a legate and, after driving back the barbarians erected another wall of turf".

Coins dating to A.D. 142 or 143 appear to commemorate a victory in Britain presumably the result of Lollius Urbicus's campaigns. The reason for the new frontier is unknown: it may have been strategic or merely to do with Antoninus Pius's need for a military success to secure his position.

In its original form, the Antonine Wall, as we now know it, appears to have been designed on similar lines to the final version of Hadrian's Wall although, as we have seen, the Wall itself was actually a turf rampart. These were to be forts at 8-mile intervals with fortlets similar to milecastles between them. A ditch ran in front of the Wall with a low mound beyond it. The only new element was a military road behind the Wall connecting the stations along it. The plan was soon changed, however, and more forts were built. The 37-mile frontier eventually had perhaps nineteen of them (only sixteen forts are known for certain) 2 miles apart. The Antonine Wall was, therefore, much more heavily garrisoned than Hadrian's Wall, having the same number of troops in half of the distance.

The construction of the Antonine Wall was marked by a remarkable series of carved and inscribed stones, or distance slabs, most of which can now be seen in the Hunterian Museum, Glasgow. They show that detachments of all three legions permanently stationed in Britain took part in the work and carefully record the lengths of Wall, measured either in paces or feet, they had been responsible for. In addition, many of them have scenes which were intended to illustrate the army's triumphs and to act as propaganda. The most dramatic is the slab from Bridgeness (in the National Museum of Antiquities, Edinburgh) which on one

ANTONINE WALL
The Roman frontier in Scotland ran from Carriden near Edinburgh on the Forth to Old Kilpatrick, a little to the north-west of Glasgow on the Clyde. To visit the sites along it travellers from the south are recommended to make first for Glasgow or Falkirk, which are some 400 miles from London.

11

side of the inscription shows a mounted cavalryman riding over four native soldiers, spear poised, and on the other a sacrifice taking place in a gabled temple. The central figure, probably the commander of the legion, dressed in a toga, stands at the altar while to one side there is a flute-player and three animals presumably awaiting ritual slaughter.

Although the evidence is difficult to interpret, it seems likely that the Antonine Wall was abandoned in about A.D. 158, possibly as a result of the need to quell a revolt in northern England. A brief period of reoccupation began in about A.D. 161 lasting to the mid-160s A.D., when a permanent withdrawal to the Hadrian's Wall frontier took place.

Five sites on the Antonine Wall illustrate particularly well the nature of the Roman Empire's most northerly frontier.

ANTONINE WALL
Watling Lodge, Central Region
OS 65 NS 862797
The site is about 1½ miles west of Falkirk town centre. Take the A803 to Glasgow, turn left just before the Forth and Clyde Canal and follow the signposts on to Tamfourhill Road. Access to both ends of the ditch is provided from the road.

The formidable rampart at Watling Lodge is now little more than half its original height.

Modern Falkirk and its suburbs have spread over much of the eastern end of the Antonine Wall, but for the traveller wishing to visit the monument there can be no better place to start than the site known as Watling Lodge. The impressive nature of the man-made barrier formed by the ditch is clearly visible here where it is something like 40 feet wide and 15 feet deep. If you remember that originally the rampart of the Wall itself towered another 10 feet above the ditch on its south side, you will realize that a Caledonian tribesman would have done more than pause for thought before attacking the might of Rome. The strategic position of the Antonine Wall may also be appreciated at this site. Soldiers based in the area would have had an excellent view of the valley of the River Carron and the Kilsyth Hills beyond it to the north.

See **Antonine Wall.**

The site at Rough Castle survives today in something of an island of unspoilt countryside surrounded by the encroachments of industry, mineral extraction and housing. There is no better place, however, to appreciate the nature of the Antonine Wall and its forts.

The fort which, at 1 acre, is one of the smallest on the Wall was probably added to it as part of the second-stage modifications to its design. According to an inscription found here, it was garrisoned by an auxiliary regiment known as the Sixth Cohort of Nervii under the command of one Flavius Betto – not an auxiliary officer, but a centurion of the Twentieth Legion. You will see that the function of the fort was clearly to overlook the valley of the River Carron to the north and, more specifically, the valley of the small Rowan Tree Burn to the west.

The fort earthworks, in the form of a double-ditch system, are better preserved here than at any other Antonine Wall site. Within the defences some bits of stonework can just be seen which represent parts of the headquarters building and a granary. To the east is the fort annexe which has three widely spaced ditches on its east side suggesting alterations to the plan during its occupation. The purpose of the annexes, which were given to all Wall forts, was to increase the area under military supervision. In this sense, they functioned something like the Vallum on Hadrian's Wall. Within the annexe there would have been room for equipment stores, stabling and that vital feature of off-duty hours, the bath house.

Before leaving Rough Castle go out of the north gate of the fort across the Wall ditch where, to your left, you will see ten rows of holes in the ground. They were ironically known as *lilia* or lilies, and originally contained camouflaged pointed stakes which were supposed to impede and confuse an enemy before he could attack the main fort defences.

For perhaps half a mile to the west and almost a mile to the east of Rough Castle, the Antonine Wall itself is very well preserved with not only the ditch but also the rampart clearly visible.

See **Antonine Wall, Antonine Wall – Bearsden**

ANTONINE WALL

Rough Castle, Central Region
OS 65 NS844798

The fort site is some 3 miles west of Falkirk town centre and may be approached either from the west or the east. From the west, take the A803 to Bonnybridge, turn left over the Forth and Clyde Canal, and then left again down a minor road signposted to the site. From the east you can take the A816 to Bonnybridge. 2 miles out of Falkirk park your car on the left by a new housing development, walk through the plantation on the north side of the road and follow the Wall ditch to the fort.

Having found and followed the Ancient Monument sign into the now largely deserted industrial wasteland, turn right at this corner for the foot of Croy Hill.

As you approach the site from Croy Village, you will soon see the Wall ditch. Keep it on your left and, as you start to climb, you will again get a good idea of the strategic position of the frontier line now overlooking the valley of the River Kelvin with good views of the Kilsyth Hills still rising majestically beyond. Little of the Wall itself survives here, but as you approach the summit of Croy Hill you will pass two low mounds which were probably the bases of signalling beacons. Communication along the Wall line to the forts was obviously vital if strategic advantage was to be turned to good effect.

You will see a natural crevice below you here, but the Wall ditch keeps to lower ground until it reaches a level platform which was the site of a small fort. Nothing can be seen of this, but it is known from inscriptions that a detachment of the Sixth Legion, normally based in York, was present here presumably engaged in construction work; and a relief from the fort, now in the National Museum of Antiquities in Edinburgh, shows three legionaries holding spears with their helmets hanging on their shields. Even their best efforts were thwarted, however, by the hardness of the rock beyond the fort and the Wall ditch was left undug for about 80 feet. After this gap, the ditch reappears and can be traced for about a mile to Dullatur.

A poignant accompaniment to your visit to Croy Hill may well be the sight of local children playing in the ditch amidst piles of rubbish and the remains of fires. It is a scene which is somehow evocative of the decay of the once-proud Roman work after the final withdrawal from Scotland in the A.D. 160s.

See **Antonine Wall.**

ANTONINE WALL

Croy Hill, Strathclyde Region
OS 64 NS 734764

The site is about 10 miles north-east of Glasgow. Approach by way of the A80 and turn left just before Cumbernauld onto the B8048. Go to the north end of Croy village and look for the Ancient Monument sign.

Spectacular views reward the traveller who tackles Croy Hill.

ANTONINE WALL

Bar Hill, Strathclyde Region
OS 64 NS 707759
The site is 9 miles north-east of Glasgow and is signposted from the main road which skirts the north end of Croy. Croy and Bar Hills are within walking distance of each other.

Bar Hill is the highest fort on the Antonine Wall line, (495 feet above sea-level) and has good views to the north, east and west, where the skyline of Glasgow is now visible. The Roman remains are not spectacular, but along with Rough Castle, it is the best site for the appreciation of what a fort on the Wall might have looked like. Unusually, however, the fort is set back from the Wall line and does not use the Wall ditch as part of its northern defences. The fort defences were otherwise similar to those of the other forts, in consisting of a double ditch and turf rampart, which would have been surmounted by a timber palisade. The ditches can most clearly be seen today on the west side of the fort and they are unbroken opposite the west gate. A bridge would have been used to cross them when required. Within the fort, the plan of the headquarters building can be traced. As usual, it consists of a basilica, with cross-hall and three offices at the back, and a courtyard.

Part of a stone-built bath can be seen in the north-west corner of the fort. Bath houses are normally found in the fort annexe but, for some reason, an exception has been made here. Other buildings, including the barracks, would have been of timber.

Two 500-strong garrisons are known from inscriptions at Bar Hill: the First Cohort of Baetasians and the First Cohort of Hamian Archers, originally from Syria, who surely did not relish the local climate. The presence of two garrisons has been taken as part of the evidence for two periods of occupation on the Antonine Wall. It is also of interest that the inscriptions were found, along with many other artefacts, in the fort well suggesting an orderly demolition here when the order came to abandon the frontier. Some of the finds may be seen in the Auld Kirk Museum, Kirkintilloch.
See **Antonine Wall, Antonine Wall – Rough Castle, The Army.**

The fort at Bearsden lay towards the west end of the Antonine Wall. It has been extensively excavated in recent years and the remains of the bath house found in the annexe on its east side form the most impressive building still to be seen on the Wall line. Its preservation is due to the good offices of the contractor responsible for the surrounding housing development.

The street which runs past the display area is on the line of the Military Way which ran through the centre of the fort and annexe, and linked it to the other installations on the Wall. When you enter the site, you are, therefore, looking at about half the original area of the annexe. The bath house before you is unusual in having a timber *apodyterium* (changing room) and *frigidarium* (cold bath). Because of the heat and damp, the rest of the bath house had to be built of stone to guard against the dangers of fire and warping

of the structure. On entering the *frigidarium* notice the cold plunge to your right, and the *laconicum* with hypocaust for sauna-type bathing on the left. Other hot rooms lie beyond. To the south-east of the baths is the latrine. The communal nature of military life extended to even the most intimate of bodily functions.

Three miles or so to the west of Bearsden fort, but also in the Glasgow suburb of that name, is Hutcheson Hill where one of the most interesting distance slabs was found. When you see it in the Hunterian Museum, Glasgow, notice, in particular, the standard bearer, with his short tunic and dagger at the belt, bowing to a personification of victory while gloomy, bound and naked captives look on. Below these scenes is a bear, the symbol of the Twentieth Legion.
See **Antonine Wall, Antonine Wall – Rough Castle.**

ANTONINE WALL

Bearsden, Strathclyde Region
OS 64 NS524727
Bearsden is a suburb of Glasgow on its north-west side. Take the A809 from the town centre and turn left in Bearsden onto the A810. The site is about 1 mile from the junction in Antonine Road, a turning on the left at the edge of the urban development.

ARDOCH

Tayside
OS 57/58 NN 839099
The site is just north of the village of Braco, 11 miles from Stirling. Approach via the A9 and then the A822 to Crieff. Park your car in Braco main street.

The fort from the north-east corner.

The earthworks at Ardoch are some of the best preserved of any fort in Britain, if not the western empire. They derive from the second and third periods of Roman occupation on the site. The earliest fort, of which no visible trace survives, belonged to the campaigns of Agricola in the early 80s and a tombstone of the period in the Hunterian Museum, Glasgow, indicates that the garrison was the First Cohort of Spaniards.

The other two forts here date from the mid-second century A.D., and served as outposts for early warning and patrolling bases for the Antonine Wall. The first fort was slightly larger than the second, suggesting that it held a larger garrison. On the north side of the present earthworks, you can clearly see where the inner rampart of the first fort has been cut by two ditches on the north side of

the second fort. The proliferation of ditches here must indicate the hostile nature of this part of Scotland, and also shows the lengths to which the army was prepared to go to protect itself. Note, however, that only one ditch was required overlooking the slope down to the River Knaik, which was presumably the fort's water supply.

North of Ardoch fort are a number of earthworks representing an annexe, and several marching camps which can be traced on a large-scale map. Some 2 miles north of Ardoch are the remains of a fortlet at Kaims and a further 4 miles on is the fort at Strageath where, at the time of writing, an excavation programme is revealing a similar sequence of occupation to that at Ardoch.
See **The Army.**

The sheer number of ditches and the complexity of their layout, make Ardoch a fascinating place to explore.

BADBURY RINGS

Dorset

OS 195 ST 965030

The Rings are about 4½ miles north-west of Wimborne and 6½ miles south-east of Blandford Forum on the B3082.

Badbury Rings today is a site with a most evocative atmosphere and well worth a visit on this account alone. It is a multi-vallate, i.e., many-ditched, hillfort of Iron Age date which may, like Hod Hill and Maiden Castle, have been one of the twenty places which, according to the Roman writer Suetonius, was stormed by the Second Legion under the general and future Emperor Vespasian, although there is no archaeological evidence for this.

The configuration of Roman roads in this area is also of some interest. Using the O.S. map, you will see that there is a junction here between a road running north-east to south-west and a road running north-west to south-east. The former is known as the Ackling

Dyke and travellers may already have seen its prominent *agger* 9 or 10 miles away near the Hampshire–Dorset border, as it makes for Old Sarum near Salisbury. The junction at the hillfort was probably the end of this road in the early years of the Roman conquest, but after perhaps ten years or so, when the army had reached Exeter, it appears to have changed alignment here to lead south-west, initially to Dorchester. The *agger* of this extension is visible on the north-west side of the Rings, and it then follows the course now occupied by a minor road going off the B3082 to the village of Shapwick, where there may have been a fort.

The other road, which passes the Rings,

Not as high-sited as some hillforts, Badbury Rings nevertheless enjoy a commanding view of the surrounding countryside.

17

originated in Hamworthy, in Poole Harbour, and heads for Bath. Hamworthy seems to have been a point of disembarkation for the Roman army at the time of the invasion in A.D. 43 and the road passes through the site of an early fortress at Lake Farm near Wimborne before reaching the hillfort. There was a small Roman settlement on the north side of Badbury Rings, but the site may have become important again in the post-Roman period as the site of King Arthur's battle of Mons Badonicus in the early sixth century. A.D. which seems to have halted the invasion of the Anglo-Saxons in this area. It has been claimed that Arthur was the last British leader to rule in the Roman tradition, and it has even been suggested that he should be seen as a British emperor. Agreeable though it is to speculate, however, the absence of firm evidence must still consign the king to the realms of myth.

See **Ackling Dyke, Roads.**

BAGINTON
Warwickshire
OS 140 SP 344752
The Lunt fort is about 2½ miles south of Coventry city centre.

The remains at many of Britain's Roman sites, where perhaps only the low rampart mound or a few wall footings survive, require the traveller to make considerable leaps of imagination if he or she is to visualize their original appearance. The only way we can usually appreciate fully the nature of vanished Roman structures is to visit the handful of places where there are full-scale reconstructions. The Lunt at Baginton is one of them and a must for all Romanists.

The first fort here was founded at the time of the Boudiccan revolt in A.D. 60, perhaps in response to the unusual military conditions of the time. It was a substantial base and its limits have not yet been established. Attention has, however, focused on the smaller fort built on the site shortly afterwards and occupied until about A.D. 80.

It was originally intended that the reconstruction would be of a typical early Roman fort, but as the excavations proceeded it soon became clear that its layout was anything but typical. One reason for this was that the defences on its eastern side described a curious sinuous course to accommodate a circular arena over 100 feet across.

The reconstruction of the defences consists, first of all, of a rampart composed of earth, derived in part from the ditch in front of it, with a sloping front and rear face made stable with blocks of turf. Since turf is plentiful in Britain, thanks to a temperate climate, the Roman troops here became experts in its use. Although an earth and turf rampart may not have the same life-span as a stone wall, the advantage of it is that it is difficult to undermine during a siege and difficult to knock down in a frontal assault. It also provides a broad fighting platform on the top where there would be a timber palisade, or "breastwork". At the Lunt this is constructed of posts driven into the rampart at intervals with a rigid paling between them. The top has crenellations which would have given the soldiers protection between bouts of throwing javelins or other projectiles.

The ditch in front of the rampart is V-shaped in profile, a *fossa fastigata* as it was known, and the inner face makes a continuous slope with the rampart. At other sites there is a platform, or berm, between the rampart base and ditch top which meant attackers were not able to hide and draw breath at the bottom.

The east gate at the Lunt has been reconstructed on the basis of representations of timber gates on Trajan's Column, a great monument erected in Rome which portrays numerous scenes of military activity and is the most important source of our knowledge for the first- and second-century A.D. Roman army. The Lunt gate has a covered area above it at rampart walkway level where, as in an interval tower, soldiers might shelter while on watch, and above this is an open platform from which missiles could be fired over a range greater than that possible from the ramparts. The measurements of many of these gateways are fairly standard, so the timbers were probably prefabricated by the army workshops and this was done again by the Royal Engineers before the replica was erected – a job which took ten men, three days using no modern equipment.

The internal fort building chosen for re-erection was a granary. In excavation its location was only indicated by rows of post holes, the details of the superstructure are unknown. One universal feature of Roman granaries, however, whether timber or stone, is a raised floor; the idea being, firstly, to allow the free circulation of air around the grain to prevent rotting and, secondly, to stop the invasion of rodents. Another recurring feature is the loading platform at one end where carts could pull up. Other than this there was not a lot to go on, but the building on the site today, which serves as the site museum, cannot be much different from the original.

The final piece of reconstruction was of the unique circular structure with a funnel-like entrance. This has been interpreted as a *gyrus*, or arena, for the training of horses and cavalrymen. The whole fort, in fact, probably served as a base for this purpose. Once the replica had been built it was discovered that one consequence of a circular wall was the enhancement of noise inside, and so it is suggested that one reason for this design was to accustom the horses to the sound level that they would encounter in battle.

The horses themselves are known from bones found in archaeological excavations and from illustrations on cavalrymen's tombstones to have been quite small, similar to our New Forest pony. The men's feet were relatively close to the ground while riding and, moreover, they had no stirrups thus making them insufficiently stable to fire arrows or throw spears with any confidence. The mounted auxiliary therefore had a sword as his principal weapon.
See **The Army.**

The four great mounds which today make up the Bartlow Barrows, or Hills as they are known locally, reflect the continuation of south-east England's late Iron Age tradition of high-status burial exemplified by the Mount and the Lexden Tumulus at Colchester. There were originally seven or eight barrows in two rows, but the western row was destroyed in 1832. The eastern row survives, but only three may be visited, the fourth being on private land north of a railway line.

All the barrows were excavated or, more exactly, tunnelled into, in the last century and human cremations were found usually contained in a wooden chest accompanied by glass, bronze and pottery vessels. In one of the barrows, a scented resin was found which was identified by none other than Michael Faraday, better known as the pioneer of electricity, as frankincense or myrrh. Faraday also examined an unusual iron chair frame from another barrow and concluded that it had had a leather seat. Unfortunately, most of the finds no longer survive as they were burnt in a fire at a local country house in 1847, but a few may be seen in Saffron Walden Museum.

Since the barrows now stand in dense woodland, travellers will find the ambience of the site quite distinctive, if not eerie.
See **Colchester.**

BARTLOW
Essex
OS 154 TL 586448
The Barrows are on the Cambridgeshire–Essex border about 10 miles south-east of Cambridge. Approach via the A604 and take the Ashdon Road in Bartlow village. There is a signpost on the left-hand side of the road just past a turning to Hadstock.

Bartlow Three Hills, as this group of barrows is known locally. The forth barrow is inaccessible some short distance away, on private land.

The Native Background
Chiefs and Celts

The first Roman invasions of Britain were those led by Julius Caesar in 55 and 54 B.C. In *De bello Gallico* (On the Gallic War), Caesar gives a detailed account of his campaigns, but has little to say on the character of the country aside from the well-known comment that, "All the Britons dye their bodies with woad, which produces a blue colour, and this gives them a more terrifying appearance in battle". Other written sources are scarce, but we know from archaeology that Britain was relatively back-ward in most respects compared with the Mediterranean world.

The nature of the Iron Age economy, based almost entirely on agri-culture, varied according to the terrain and climate, a major divide being between the more fertile and temperate "lowland zone" lying roughly south-east of a line from Exeter to York, and the harsher "highland zone" north-west of it. Economic conditions affected society, but at the time of Caesar Britain's people were basically grouped under chiefdoms where power was based on inheritance through family lineage, but whose spheres of influence were constantly shifting according to the fortunes of internecine war. We know the names of many native chiefdoms from classical sources and because they were converted into what we might call self-governing tribal homelands after the conquest. Ethnically, the majority of natives may be referred to as Celtic, although the term is difficult to define except in terms of language and artistic styles.

After the invasions of Caesar, contacts between Britain and the Euro-pean continent grew and this was to have a profound effect on the people living in the south and east of the country. Two trade routes were particu-larly important: one between northern France and Dorset, concentrated on a port at Hengistbury Head near Poole and the other between the mouth of the Rhine and the area around the Thames estuary. Trade meant an increasing familiarity with Roman culture and in the south-east was accompanied by the arrival of new settlers known as the Belgae.

The Belgic people, who called themselves the Catuvellauni, gradually assumed dominance over others in the south and east including the Atrebates of Hampshire, Sussex and Berkshire. This process can be traced by a study of the distribution of coins, which now begin to be minted in quantity in Britain for the first time, and other cultural traits, including the use of the potter's wheel and the burial practice of richly furnished cremation. The basis of the Catuvellauni's success was prob-ably their control over rich grain-producing areas which yielded sufficient surplus for a lucrative cross-channel trade, with the Roman army as, perhaps, the major customer; it is surely no accident that the wheat sheaf is a common feature on their coins.

This economic development permitted the growth of a complex society ruled by a warrior aristocracy and the power of the Catuvellauni reached its height in the reigns of King Cunobelin, who died about A.D. 40, and his sons, Caratacus and Togodumnus. One of their principal centres was the "fort of the war god Camulos", or Camulodunum near Colchester, where major dyke systems protected a large area containing temples, an industrial site and a possible royal enclosure. A similar site existed near St Albans. We should remember, however, that the vast majority of the population lived in peasant settlements which ranged from single farms with one or two huts to larger villages.

While the south-east was developing rapidly, the area of Wessex further west fell behind. The trade route through Hengistbury declined, and politically people were less unified. As a result, there may have been more intertribal conflict which explains the continued occupation of hill-forts such as Hod Hill and Maiden Castle in the territory of the Durotriges.

The people of the highland zone seem to have been largely untouched by events in the south-east, and their way of life changed very little. In many parts they lived in hillforts, although villages similar to those in the lowlands are also known. In the north of England territory of the Brigantes, however, hillforts are rare and the pattern is of scattered pastoral settlement. The great enclosure at Stanwick may perhaps be seen as an unusual response to the unprecedented situation of Roman aggression.

In spite of the increasingly Romanized tastes of the Catuvellaunian leadership, they were firmly anti-Roman politically and probably provided help for would-be rebels in neighbouring Gaul. To the imperial government, this was intolerable and an excuse for intervention in Britain may have been provided by the flight of Verica, King of the Atrebates, to Rome and his appeal for help against the Catuvellauni. A number of other reasons for the invasion of A.D. 43 may be advanced, however, including the Emperor Claudius's need for a military triumph to secure his position and a desire to acquire Britain's economic resources. The Greek geographer Strabo writing at this time refers to this country as a source of grain, cattle, gold, silver, iron, hides, slaves and hunting dogs.

The Britons were ill-equipped to meet the Roman challenge. Their troops were largely poorly organized, apart perhaps from the charioteers who, Caesar noted, trained regularly. All the Britons really had to offer against the 40,000 men of Aulus Plautius, the Roman commander, was the courage born of a will to retain their independence.

See **Colchester, Hod Hill, Maiden Castle, Temples and Religion.**

At first sight, the Roman temple and spa complex at Bath appear to be a piece of pure classical civilization transplanted to Britain from the Mediterranean but, on closer examination, the atmosphere created by the merging of the Roman goddess, Minerva, with the presiding Celtic god, Sulis, assumes a distinctly local flavour.

The native Britons commonly attributed divinity to water – whether as spring, stream, or river – and so it is not surprising that the hot springs of Bath were treated as sacred before the arrival of the Romans, who were themselves great respecters of local deities in conquered lands and were doubtless impressed by the magical appearance of hot water from the ground and its curative properties. In the 60s and 70s, therefore, building on the site began, clearly under official supervision at the highest level. At great expense, masons, sculptors and other craftsmen would have been brought from abroad to create the splendid buildings and their internal appointments. Altars dedicated by legionaries here also suggest official sponsorship for Bath.

The Roman structures visible today are not easy to understand, since to see them it is necessary to undergo the disorienting effect of going below the floor level of the Georgian Pump Room. Essentially, however, you can visit most of the baths, the spring source and the south-east corner of the temple precinct which lay on the north-west side of the baths.

On entering the museum, you pass the west end of the spring now known as the King's Bath, and after descending you are soon confronted with the great temple pediment. Its centrepiece, a male gorgon's face on the shield of Sulis – Minerva, is carved in a vigorous style mixing Celtic and Classical motifs. A more formal head of Minerva in bronze can also be seen in the Museum which must have belonged to an important cult statue. It was dug up in 1727 and since then research into the history of Aquae Sulis has been a continuing process.

The spring itself was originally contained within a polygonal reservoir open to the air, but in the later second century A.D. it was enclosed in a vaulted chamber which must have created a mysterious grotto-like effect. This did not prevent the continued deposition of votive offerings in the spring, however, and many of them are on display to the visitor. There are large numbers of coins, but look out also for jewellery and metal vessels, known as *paterae*. The spring has also yielded a number of curses written on rolled-up lead plates which are usually messages from the discontented hoping to enlist the goddess's help in bringing unpleasant punishments to those who have done them wrong in some way, usually by stealing their clothing, jewellery, money, or other property.

Within the temple precinct, you can inspect the steps which led up to the temple podium. The first building was constructed in pure classical style with the entrance to the shrine behind four pillars, topped with Corinthian capitals, supporting the pediment. In the later second century A.D., contemporary with the enclosure of the spring, the temple was reconstructed with a raised ambulatory around it and two small shrines either side of the steps to give an overall effect more akin to the Romano-Celtic type of temple.

In the precinct to the east of the temple, you will see the north wall of the spring building, in the centre of which is the base of a doorway. Buttresses at each end of the wall indicate the problems of stability in damp ground. Opposite the doorway, and originally visible through it from across the spring, is the open-air sacrificial altar – a stone block with carvings of gods from the classical pantheon at each corner. Bacchus, Hercules and Jupiter can still be seen. To one side of the altar is an inscription, on what is probably a statue base, recording the gift of Marcius Memor, a *haruspex*, or auguren, whose duty it was to sacrifice animals on the altar and, with due ceremony, to examine the entrails.

To the north of the altar stood the Facade of the Four Seasons, so-called because of the carvings on it which included this popular Roman theme. The central panel, however, bore a representation of Luna, the Moon Goddess and, appropriately the doorway to the spring opposite was probably surmounted by a representation of Sol, the Sun God. A cosmic balance was thereby created.

After viewing the remains of the Facade, you pass out of the temple precinct and arrive at the Great Bath, passing on the way a collection of sculpture from the site. Notice, in particular, the altar set up for the well-being of Aufidius Maximus, a centurion of the Sixth Legion. The Great Bath itself never fails to capture the imagination, although you should appreciate that in Roman times it would have been roofed with a great masonry vault cunningly constructed of hollow tiles to reduce its weight. To the west, there was originally a suite of artificially heated baths. In the early second century A.D., the baths complex was extended – perhaps because of Hadrian's decree forbidding mixed bathing – a new suite of heated baths was built at the east end of the Great Bath, and there was also new work at the west end including the installation of an impressive circular plunge.

At the end of the Roman period, this monument to gracious living was simply left to decay until perhaps the seventh century A.D. when parts were evidently deliberately dismantled. Its sad appearance in the eighth century A.D. is apparently described in a poem called "The Ruin", which begins:

Wondrous is the wall-stone;
broken by fate,
the castles have decayed; the work
of giants is crumbling.

See **Temples and Religion.**

23

BEADLAM

North Yorkshire
OS 100 SE 634 842

The villa is 1½ miles east of Helmsley on the A170. When you reach a crossroads with a left turn for Pockley, the site is in the field on your right. Beadlam village is 1 mile further east.

Beadlam is the only Roman villa of which anything substantial can be seen in the north of England. It forms one of a group which occupied the rich agricultural land of east Yorkshire. Outside this area, villas are sparse in the north reflecting the relatively poor prospects for farming in largely upland country and, no doubt, the backwardness of the native population in adopting Roman ways. Beadlam, like the other Yorkshire villas, is, moreover, in no way comparable in its size or appointments to some of the great villas, such as Chedworth or Bignor, in the south.

Excavations have not been exhaustive here, so all we know is that in the fourth century A.D. the villa consisted of two distinct rectangular buildings at right angles to each other facing a courtyard. The remains of the west building have been backfilled, but the north building has been left exposed. The entrance was in the middle of the south side, and in a room facing south near the east end there was a mosaic which has now been removed, revealing a hypocaust underneath – a haven for rabbits at the time of writing. Another room with a hypocaust is to be seen at the west end of the building which was heated from the room east of it; between the two is a well-preserved flue arch.

The site has a most agreeable aspect, there is water in a stream a little to the east of the site and stone suitable for building outcrops a little to the north. The owner of Beadlam will probably never be identified, but he may have been a legionary veteran turned farmer from York or a local man who had prospered on trade in farm products with that city.
See **York, Villas.**

BIGNOR

Sussex
OS 197 SU 987146

The villa is about 14 miles north-east of Chichester via the A27 and A29. Look for a minor road in the village of Bury.

In the later third and early fourth centuries A.D., the countryside in much of Roman Britain seems to have enjoyed an unprecedented prosperity and this is reflected in the growth of Romanized farms or villas. The developments at Bignor in the pleasant downland of Sussex are typical of the period. The first stone-built, or partly stone-built house, a simple rectangle in plan, succeeded a timber structure in the mid-third century A.D. A little later, projecting wings were added to it to give extra space and a more impressive façade. In the later third century A.D., the whole establishment was expanded on a grand scale. The original house was rebuilt and the great north and south wings added so as to enclose a large courtyard on three sides. Extensive farm buildings are known to exist to the east, and successful agriculture was doubtless the basis of the owner's wealth. The urban market at Chichester was only a few miles to the south-west along a Roman road known as Stane Street which passes close to the villa.

We know little about the owner and his family, but like other members of the upper classes in Britain at this time, he was probably something of a man of letters with a keen interest in mythology and philosophical speculation, judging by a fine group of mosaics laid here in the early fourth century A.D. Pride of place is perhaps taken by one which shows the abduction of the beautiful Prince Ganymede by Jupiter disguised as an

The fine mosaics at Bignor are superbly displayed within their custom-built surroundings which include an informative museum, coffee shop and extensive car parking facilities.

eagle. In compensation for making him his bedfellow, Jupiter allowed Ganymede to become immortal and the significance of the mosaic, to those who admired it originally, may have been that it symbolized the soul's journey from this terrestrial life of care to one of eternal joy in the heavens. In the same room there are also six panels showing dancing girls surrounding a *piscina*, or water-basin. *See* **Brading, Lullingstone, Villas.**

Room 7 at Bignor, with its hexagonal water basin and mosaic floor.

One of the most striking testimonies to the political upheavals of the fourth century A.D. is the great man-made bank and ditch known as Bokerley Dyke, which stretches for nearly 4 miles along the Hampshire – Dorset border across part of Salisbury Plain. At each end, it terminates in upland areas which would have been forested in Roman times and are still wooded today.

The first phase of the ditch was constructed in about A.D. 330 and comes to within 500 yards of the east side of the modern A354. Initially, its purpose was probably to protect the rich pastures of north-east Dorset from marauders. This land may have been part of an imperial estate, that is land under the direct control of the state, farmed to supply the army and administration.

At some time between A.D. 364 and A.D. 370, the Dyke was extended westwards across the line of the A354 and, more importantly, across the Roman road known as Ackling Dyke, which was now blocked. This may well have been a reaction to the great *Barbarica Conspiratio* (Barbarian Conspiracy) referred to by the contemporary writer Ammianus Marcellinus, which shook Britain in A.D. 367. In this year all the barbarian tribes who had been harassing the country since the middle of the century managed to unite, and the result was anarchy and chaos. The Roman response was to send a general known as Count Theodosius to restore Britain's defences and, once peace was restored, the road was reopened.

At the very end of the fourth century A.D., the western dyke was replaced by another a little to the north in a better strategic position. It also interrupted the road line, but there was no subsequent restoration. This dyke may be the work of one Flavius Stilicho, who, in the mid-390s, was the last Roman official to attempt to secure the empire's hold on this country.

The dating of these dykes is largely the work of one of the fathers of British archaeology, General Pitt-Rivers, who owned much of the surrounding land known as Cranborne Chase. He had the sort of luck all archaeologists need, for in 1888 the conductor of his private band was apparently strolling along the Dyke and, in a hole dug by a local farmer, found five datable coins and a brooch. A walk along the Dyke is still to be recommended, but it is unlikely that you will make a comparable discovery, and please do not dig any holes!
See **Ackling Dyke, Roads.**

BOKERLEY DYKE
Dorset/Hampshire
OS 184 SU 055181
The best way to get to the Dyke is on the A354 which it crosses at Woodyates, some 13 miles south-west of Salisbury. A right of way runs along the Dyke but you may have to scale the roadside fence.

Suetonius records that Vectis, as the Isle of Wight was known in Roman times, was subjugated by Vespasian as he moved westwards, with the Second Augustan Legion, through the south of England. There is no record of any resistance by the natives and, subsequently, the island seems to have become a peaceful and prosperous agricultural area. It was not a complete backwater, however, for in the early-fourth century A.D. mosaic pavements laid at Brading Villa there is remarkable evidence for a man who, like the owner of Bignor Villa, had the most sophisticated philosophical and literary interests. His preoccupations appear to reflect the intellectual climate of the time, focusing as they do on the search for divinity through esoteric revelation and spiritual ecstasy.

The most complex mosaic displays a considerable awareness of classical literature and may depict, in allegorical form, aspects of the search for eternal life through victory over death and evil. In the central roundel, there is a picture of the gorgon, Medusa, with splendid snaky hair, whose gaze turned men to stone and from whom Perseus rescued Andromeda. In surrounding panels, there are scenes from other myths which show Ceres giving seed to Triptolemos, who taught the world agriculture (appropriate for a villa); Lycurgus in pursuit of Ambrosia who, to save herself, prayed to Bacchus who, in response, changed her into a vine which then strangled her pursuer; a shepherd admiring a girl playing a tambourine; and a nymph pursued by a man. Between these scenes are personifications of the four winds and on other panels are representations of mermaids and tritons, and a picture of an astronomer pointing to a globe who may symbolize Knowledge through which salvation is achieved.

Another mosaic has Bacchus in the centre, a god associated with ecstatic and sensual rites. To one side, there is a most unusual scene featuring a cock-headed figure standing beside a ladder leading up to a house. The meaning of this is far from clear, but it may show the straight and narrow path to salvation in god's house. There are also two griffins here, presumably representing the evil demons who beset our earthly lives.

A third mosaic depicts Orpheus, who is known on a number of pavements from Britain, charming the birds and the beasts, as usual, with his magic lyre. The significance of the theme to the *cognoscenti* was probably in its allegorical value, however, since Orpheus was a principal figure in another death and rebirth myth. On the demise of his wife, Eurydice, he was forced to search for her in Tartarus, the underworld, where he had to charm the ferryman Charon, the dog Cerberus, and the Judges of the Dead with his music before she could be recovered.
See **Bignor, Lullingstone, Villas**

BRADING
Isle of Wight
OS 196 SZ 599862
Brading is on the east side of the Isle of Wight about 3½ miles south of Ryde.

The Army
Continuity and Change

The Roman army which conquered Britain was one of the most successful military machines the world has ever known. Its success, like that of any good army, was based on discipline, organization and the flair of its commanders.

The élite troops of the early Imperial Army were the legions. Each one consisted of some 6,000 men of whom about 5,300 were heavy infantry; the rest included clerks, specialist craftsmen and mounted scouts. The basic unit of infantry was the *contubernium* of eight men who shared a tent while on campaign. Ten *contubernia* made up a century (80 men) and six centuries formed a cohort (480 men). Ten cohorts made up a legion but the First Cohort was of double strength, hence the total of about 5,300.

The legion was commanded by a *legatus* (legate), a man of senatorial rank who had previously served as praetor, that is, a magistrate in Rome, and was directly answerable to the emperor through the provincial governor. Under the legate, there were six military tribunes headed by a *tribunus laticlavius*, a young man of senatorial rank destined for high office. His military experience, however, would have been limited and real command of the troops lay with the centurions. In recognition of their importance, centurions were paid over fifteen times more than the ordinary legionary. Another important post in the century was the *signifer*, or standard bearer; the first Roman soldier on British soil was probably a *signifer* of Julius Caesar's Tenth Legion who jumped ashore while his comrades hesitated.

Legionaries were recruited from Roman citizens only. In the invasion force of A.D. 43, therefore, there were a significant number of Italians, if not actual Romans, but as a result of the gradual extension of citizenship, most legionaries, by the later first century A.D. were probably non-Italian provincials. Each man signed on for twenty-five years and before the reign of Septimius Severus, he was forbidden to marry formally until his discharge when he might be given cash or a grant of land in a *colonia*.

The legionary's weapons consisted primarily of a javelin and a sword used for thrusting in close combat. To protect himself, he wore a helmet and body armour made of overlapping metal strips and carried a large rectangular shield.

Since the structure of a legion was fairly standard, so too was the layout of a fortress. It had a "playing-card" shape and was roughly 50 acres in extent. In the centre was the *principia*, or headquarters building. It consisted of an outer courtyard and was surrounded on three sides by a verandah and offices. On the fourth side lay the basilica, an aisled hall where the whole legion could be addressed by its commander from the raised *tribunal* at one end. Beyond the hall lay five rooms, one of which served as the treasury and the central room, or *aedes*, was a shrine where the standards were kept along with an image of the divine emperor. Passing in front of the *principia* between the two side gates was the *via principalis*, one of the fortress's main streets and in front of the *principia* it met the *via praetoria* which ran up from the main gate, the *porta praetoria*. The central range of buildings facing the *via principalis* might include, in addition to the *principia*, the *praetorium*, or commanding officer's house, the bath house, the hospital and the barracks of the First Cohort. On the opposite side of the street lay the houses of the six military tribunes. The rest of the fortress was occupied by barracks which were arranged as opposing pairs. Each *contubernium* had two rooms: one for sleeping in and one for equipment. At the end of the barracks, there were slightly larger quarters for the centurion.

Fortress defences in Britain consisted initially of a ditch and earthen rampart, revetted with sloping faces of stacked turves, surmounted by a palisade. The gates and internal towers were also made of timber. In due course, the permanent legionary fortresses in Britain at Chester, Caerleon and York were rebuilt throughout in stone.

The legionaries were supported by auxiliary troops who were non-citizens from conquered territories. They were formed into units 500 or 100 strong, of cavalry (*alae*) infantry (*cohortes peditatae*) or part-mounted infantry (*cohortes equitatae*). The names of the units usually indicate the area in which they were originally recruited before being moved around the empire to serve. Local recruitment would then soon dilute their original character, but one only has to look at a list of the auxiliary regiments serving in Britain to appreciate the truly cosmopolitan nature of the Roman Empire. Since an auxiliary would be awarded citizenship on discharge, military service was an important route to social advancement for the subject peoples.

Auxiliaries were less heavily armed than the legionaries. They usually carried smaller circular shields, a sword and a dagger but sometimes had specialist weapons, like the Syrian archers at Carvoran fort on Hadrian's Wall. Cavalrymen would adorn their horses with attractive bridle fittings in styles probably reflecting their regional origins.

Large numbers of auxiliary forts are known in Britain, Agricola alone probably founded over 100. The most instructive today are at Caernafon, Chesters, Hardknott and Housesteads. In the early Roman period, they were essentially miniature versions of a fortress, although the bath house always lay outside the defences. Fort size varied according to the size of the garrison so that on Hadrian's Wall, for example, Greatchesters was only 3·36 acres while Stanwix (Carlisle) is 9·32.

In addition to forts, a large number of smaller military posts are known, including the milecastles on Hadrian's Wall and fortlets like Castle Greg in Scotland, which were principally used for policing local tribesmen. While on campaign, the army would also construct temporary "marching camps" which simply consisted of a bank and ditch defence enclosing sufficient space for the tents. Finally, to train troops in the construction of fortifications, practice camps were created of which the best examples are at Cawthorn.

The structure and organization of the Roman army was never static and by the early fourth century A.D., it was a very different force to that which had conquered Britain in the first century A.D. A major change, probably the work of Constantine, was the removal of the army from the control of the provincial governor. It, therefore, became unnecessary to base army commands in particular provinces, which gave the emperor greater flexibility in his troop movements. Secondly, the troops were divided into two categories: the mobile field army, *comitatenses*, largely mounted; and the frontier troops, *limitanei*, descendants of the legions who had become fossilized on the periphery of an empire which had ceased to expand.

Late Roman fortifications reflect new military attitudes. The prime consideration was now defence, as opposed to offence which had prevailed in the first and second centuries A.D.. Throughout the western empire, there were forts built like those on the "Saxon Shore" with free-standing stone walls and bastions for artillery, which served as strong points to resist invasion rather than as temporary staging posts on the route to further conquest.

We know a good deal about military organization and disposition in the fourth century A.D., thanks to a document known as the *Notitia dignitatum* which dates to about A.D. 395. Many of the units listed in it probably contained mercenary troops from outside the empire whose loyalties were uncertain. By sacrificing patriotism for expediency, the Roman army was sowing the seeds of the empire's destruction.

See **Baginton, Burgh Castle Caerleon, Caernafon, Hadrian's Wall – Chesters and Housesteads, Hardknott, Portchester Castle.**

Portchester Castle.

The surviving guardroom at the east gate.

Most of Wales was initially hostile to the Romans. The Welsh tribes were encouraged in their enmity by Caratacus, one of the sons of King Cunobelin of the Catuvellauni who fled to the Silures of south Wales after the Roman conquest of his homeland in south-east England. Caratacus was eventually handed over to the Romans by Queen Cartimandua of the Brigantes in about A.D. 70, but it was not until the mid-70s, that the governor Frontinus was able to turn containment of the Welsh into conquest.

The settlement of south Wales was based on the fortress at Caerleon. From here, a network of roads spread out linking forts which controlled river valleys and other lines of communication with a view to breaking up

the native population into manageable units. Brecon Gaer is one of those forts and you can see the excellent strategic eye of the Roman commander who has chosen a site in a small plateau overlooking the valley of the Usk to the south and of the smaller River Ysgir to the west.

This is the largest Roman fort in Wales. Today it is kept as a field and one may see sheep peacefully grazing where once a garrison of 500 Spanish cavalry of the auxiliary Ala Vettonum went about their business. Excavations were undertaken here by the great British archaeologist, Sir Mortimer Wheeler, who showed that the earliest fort was defended by a bank and ditch and had timber buildings within it, but that during the

BRECON GAER
(Cicurium)
Powys
OS 160 SO 004296
The fort is some 3 miles west of Brecon. The best approach is by way of a minor road running north-west from Brecon to Cradoc. Turn left here towards Aberyscir, and then take the second left up a narrow road to Y Gaer farm. Here, it is polite to ask permission to visit the site which lies beyond the farmyard.

31

reign of the Emperor Trajan, perhaps in about A.D. 105, the defences and buildings were rebuilt in stone. This pattern is repeated at a number of Welsh forts and indicates that after a period of assessment, the army decided to make the pattern of occupation permanent.

The fort wall survives at its best on the north side, where it is still 11 feet high with up to twelve courses of facing stones surviving in places. The north-east turret is also well preserved. At the east gate, only one guardroom is visible, but the south gate is of considerable interest. It had a double portal with a guardroom on either side; the still survives in the western carriageway and a drain which ran underneath it is exposed. The west gate is unusual in having projecting guard chambers: note the pivot holes for the gate itself.

In the late Roman period the garrison appears to have been much reduced, so much so that there was room to build a bath suite inside the fort. Occupation petered out at the end of the fourth century A.D., but the place had a lasting influence on the area. It would have been a Roman road that brought the Celtic chieftain, Brychan, to the area where he was to found the petty kingdom of Brycheiniog, which became Brecknock, until recently the county name. Brychan's grandson, St Cynidr, is reputed to have been the first Christian missionary in these parts.
See **Caerleon, The Army.**

The remnants of the turret at the east end of Brecon Gaer's great north wall.

BURGH CASTLE

(Gariannonum)
Norfolk
OS 134 TG 475045
The fort is about 4 miles from Great Yarmouth town centre. Take the Lowestoft Road, and Burgh Castle is signposted at the first roundabout.

Burgh Castle is one of Britain's so-called "Saxon Shore" forts. The term Saxon Shore, or *litus saxonicum*, comes from a document known as the *Notitia Dignitatum*, which dates from the end of the fourth century A.D. This is a very important source for Romano-British history, as it lists the country's military posts, garrisons and principal commands among which there is a count, or *comes*, of the Saxon Shore. We do not know how long the Saxon Shore had been thought of as a single command, but it is likely that a system of coherent defences along the south and east coast of Britain had developed since the early third century A.D. to combat the threat of seaborne raiders.

The earliest forts in the system were probably at Brancaster (Norfolk) and Reculver, but there seems to have been a spate of fort building in the last quarter of the third century A.D., possibly as a response to the great barbarian incursion into Gaul in A.D. 276. Burgh Castle belongs to this period along with Dover, Richborough and Lympne. Burgh itself is some 4 miles from the sea at Yarmouth and stands on the bank of the Breydon Water, estuary of the River Waveney, which was evidently rather wider in Roman times.

You will find that, architecturally, the Saxon Shore forts differ from early Roman forts because their walls are free-standing with no substantial ramparts behind them, and because they are less regular in plan. Burgh, however, is interesting because it still has the rounded corners of an early fort, whereas Richborough, for example, has the rectangular corners typical of a later fort. You will also see that Burgh has external bastions around the walls, a late Roman feature, but it is possible that they were not part of the original design. If you look carefully at the point where the bastions join the curtain wall, you will see that they are not bonded to them for the lower few feet. At some stage soon after construction started, it would seem that there was a change of plan.

The purpose of the bastions was to support

ballistae, or large military catapults, which could throw iron bolts or stone balls with ferocious accuracy for up to 400 yards. If you look at the fallen bastion on the south side of the fort, you can see a socket at the top for anchoring the base of the *ballista*. The operation of these machines must have been one of the skills of the Equites Stablesiani Gariannonensium which the *Notitia Dignitatum* records as the garrison here.

Today the walls survive more or less to their full height on three sides, the riverside wall having disappeared. The original facing of flints with tile bands is especially well preserved on the south side. There is only one original gateway, a single opening in the east wall.

The garrison was probably withdrawn in A.D. 407–8 by Constantine III, a would-be usurper of the imperial crown, who needed all the troops he could muster in Gaul. Burgh reappears in history, however, as the site of a seventh-century A.D. monastery founded by the Irish monk, St Fursey, and again as a Norman castle whose mound can be seen in the south-west corner. The presence of these two establishments probably accounts for the good survival of the Roman walls.
See **Dover, Lympne, Richborough, The Army.**

The fortress at Caerleon, a Welsh word for "City of the Legions", was the headquarters of some 5,000 heavy infantry belonging to the Second Augustan Legion. Isca, as the Romans called it, after the nearby river now known as the Usk, was founded in about A.D. 75 by the governor Frontinus as a base for the consolidation of Rome's hold on south Wales. The 50-acre site had the standard fortress layout with buildings initially of timber and defences consisting, at first, of a ditch and turf rampart surmounted by a palisade. In the early second century A.D., probably after A.D. 130, when the troops returned from work on Hadrian's Wall, reconstruction of buildings and defences alike was undertaken in stone as Caerleon became one of Britain's three permanent legionary stations.

The *principia* of the fortress lay roughly where the church in the present village now stands. In the next *insula* to the south-east, stood the baths. In forts, baths are usually found outside the defences but in a fortress there is space to accommodate them within. The excavated remains are now to be seen in a splendid new building with audio-visual equipment and clear concise labels and wall panels. As you enter, you will see a large open-air swimming pool – a rare feature in this country but comparable to one in the town baths at Wroxeter. Beyond it is a heated changing room and part of the *frigidarium*, including three cold plunges, two of which are apsed and one rectangular. The carved drain cover here is especially fine. Both the *frigidarium* and other principal halls in the baths would originally have been most impressive with their roofs spanned by vaults

CAERLEON
(Isca)
Gwent
O3 171 3T 340905
Caerleon is some 6 miles north-east of Newport town centre on the B4596. You can park your car outside the Baths Museum in the centre of the village.

The remains of huge butresses testify to the scale of the stone-clad earth banks they once supported.

The one time open-air swimming pool at Caerleon.

at, perhaps, a height of some 50 feet. Finally, notice the fragment of mosaic on display which shows the tip of a spear adapted as a Bacchic "wand" with leaves and streamers wrapped around it and used, according to legend, to deter intruders on the revels of the god and his followers.

In the north-west corner of the fortress, now known as Prysg field, the stone footings of four barrack blocks are visible. Three are reconstructions but one is original and, therefore, the only fortress barrack of which anything can still be seen in Britain. In usual fashion, the barracks are arranged in pairs which face inwards onto a common street. They are broken up into double rooms which each accommodated eight men. Curiously, however, there are twelve of these rooms, two more than strictly required for a cohort – the spares were possibly occupied by some of the many specialist adminstrators or technicians attached to a legion. The larger rooms at the end of the barracks were for the centurions.

The defences can also be seen close by and include the north-west corner tower and an internal tower. Another classic feature of fortress layout is the ovens dug into the back of the rampart. The defences remain visible down to the south-east corner of the fortress and beyond the west gate, or *porta*

principialis dextra, stone walling survives.

Just outside the walls is the famous amphitheatre, the only fully excavated example in Britain, which was built between A.D. 80 and A.D. 90, making it contemporary with the Colosseum in Rome, of which it is a somewhat humbler version. It was constructed by hollowing out the central arena and using the upcast soil as banks, or *cavea,* for seating. The banks were encased in stone walls which have had to be heavily buttressed in places to bear the weight. Visitors cannot but be also impressed by the height of the surviving walls and by the appearance of the two main entrances which lack only their vaults to render them complete. Six other breaks in the *cavea* were for steps up to the seating, *vomitoria* as they were called, and on each side of the arena is a small room where performers, beasts, or prisoners might await their cue. One of them has a small brick shrine in which an altar to Nemesis may have stood and one of the most well-known finds from Caerleon is the "Gladiator's Curse". It is written on a small lead plate and has been translated as, "Lady Nemesis, I give you this cloak and boots. Let him who wore them not redeem them save by the life of his *sanguineus" Sanguineus* has been translated as chestnut horse, although there are other

Caerleon's Bath Museum conveys the impression of an art gallery. Above, the Bacchic "wand" mosaic, far left, a skillfully pierced drainage cover, and left, a carved representation of the head of Medusa, the Gorgon.

possibilities. In any event, the gladiator was clearly using a common magical practice to gain power over a rival through cursing his clothes. If successful, either the rival or his horse would die thanks to the goddess's intervention.

The size of the amphitheatre is such that it could seat the legion at full strength and was probably used for the performance of the many compulsory religious ceremonies required of it, as well as for military drill. As the curse implies, however, relaxation in the presence of some of the bloodthirsty sports for which Rome is notorious was also part of a soldier's life.

Caerleon declined in importance in the later third century A.D. and the Second Legion was at Richborough in the fourth, but the site has remained of historical significance and is associated in legend with King Arthur's deeds. Local tradition refers to the amphitheatre as "King Arthur's Round Table" and the poet Tennyson came here to write his famous epic about Arthur, "The Idylls of the King".

See **Brecon Gaer, Chester, The Army, Public Buildings.**

CAERNAFON

(Seqontium)
Gwynedd
OS 115 SH 485624
Caernafon is 246 miles from London. To reach it, use the M1 to Birmingham and then the M54 and A5 to Bangor. Near Bangor, the A5 joins the A55 which reaches Caernafon after only a few miles. The town is dominated by the medieval castle – scene of the investiture of the Prince of Wales. Travellers in the area should also see the Roman walls at Holyhead in Anglesey.

As you stand in the fort at Caernafon, with Snowdon visible behind you on a clear day, it is, perhaps, difficult to imagine that the shores of the island of Anglesey in the distance across the Menai Straits were witness to one of the most dramatic events in the conquest of Britain. But in that most eventful year, A.D. 60, the army of the governor Suetonius Paulinus, in its attempt to conquer the local tribe, known as the Ordovices, was confronted by a scene described by Tacitus as follows: "The enemy lined the shore in a dense armed mass. Among them were black-robed women with dishevelled hair like Furies, brandishing torches. Close by stood Druids, raising their hands to heaven and screaming dreadful curses." The Romans eventually prevailed, of course, but, because of the revolt of Boudicca, had to retreat rapidly from the area and only returned during the governorship of Agricola in A.D. 78 or 79. The Ordovices were then quickly defeated and Welsh resistance was at an end. An unusual relic of the Agricolan period is to be seen in the site museum: it is a piece of leather which probably comes from a tent used by his troops while on campaign.

The fort at Caernafon established by Agricola was defended by a ditch and earthen rampart surmounted by a timber palisade. Its garrison of 1,000 men evidently included cavalry for a bugler, necessary component of a cavalry regiment, named Januarius is known from a graffiti scratched by him on a pot. This can also be seen in the museum. The regiment itself may have been the First Cohort of Vardulli from Spain.

Since Caernafon lies on the sea and was a pivotal point in the road system, it had a vital place in the army's communication system which accounts for its continuous occupation throughout the Roman period, unlike many Welsh forts which were abandoned in the second century A.D. By about A.D. 140, the internal buildings and defences had, like those at Brecon Gaer, been reconstructed in stone. It is of interest that the stone used in the headquarters and some other buildings is Cheshire sandstone, which must have been brought here by water and

suggests that a legionary detachment from Chester did the building work.

The buildings, gates and defensive wall visible today are partly second century A.D. but also include work of the third and fourth centuries A.D. By the end of the second century A.D., the garrison was apparently reduced to 500 men, the regiment now being the Sunici from the Rhineland. They were apparently responsible for the construction of a Mithraic temple outside the fort and an altar from it can be seen in the museum. This reduction in garrison meant that, again as at Brecon Gaer, there was room to construct a bath house inside the fort and this can be seen on the south side of the modern road, which bisects the site, west of a more substantial bath house which dates from the later third or fourth century A.D. Possibly dating from this latter period also is a stretch of wall known as Hen Waliau, which can be found in the garden of the house called Bron Hendre at the bottom of the hill north of the fort. This is probably part of a fortified landing point and indicates growing insecurity on the Welsh coast in the late Roman times probably as a result of barbarian raids from across the Irish Sea.

In the mid-fourth century A.D., the Segontium garrisons may have been taken by the usurper Magnentius for service elsewhere and there is evidence for damage to the fort at this time. Although some restoration was evidently undertaken, perhaps by Theodosius, in about A.D. 369, the garrison was probably finally depleted by another would-be usurper, Magnus Maximus. Although there is no evidence that he was Welsh, Magnus Maximus is an important figure in Welsh legend where he is referred to as Macsen Wledig and many Dark Age Welsh kings traced their ancestry to him.

Finally, while you are in the museum, be sure to look at a very unusual gold talisman, a replica, inscribed in Greek letters and magical symbols. This was probably kept rolled up and may have been worn for luck by some superstitious member of the garrison.
See **Brecon Gaer, The Army, Emperors in Britain.**

CAERWENT

(Venta Silurum)
Gwent
OS 171 ST 469905
The village of Caerwent is about 14 miles east of Newport on the A48; or 21 miles west of Bristol, using the M4 to Chepstow and then the A48.

The walls of Caerwent are one of the most striking remains of Roman Britain. They survive up to 17 feet high on the south side of the town, only a little short of their original size. Since the modern village is small, extensive excavations within the walls have been possible and they have determined much of the internal layout. A plan is displayed outside the church which shows, amongst other things, that the main Roman street, which was also the Gloucester – Caerleon road, lies under and was rather wider than the main village street.

Caerwent may have begun life as a fort, but after the pacification of the local Silures tribe,

it becomes one of Wales' two tribal, or *civitas,* capitals (the other is Carmarthen). Important testimony to the way *civitas* government was carried out can be found in an inscription now in the church porch, in honour of Tiberius Claudius Paulinus who, amongst other things, had been commander of the Second Legion at nearby Caerleon and it commemorates the erection, probably of a statue, by the *ordo* of the *civitas Silurum –* the ruling body of the Silures tribe. The wording shows that in what we might call the tribal homelands, no legal distinction between urban and rural dwellers existed comparable to that between the inhabitants of the

Walls and turret on the south side of the Roman town.

Caerwent provides clear evidence of how the Romans constructed their town walls.

chartered towns and those living outside them.

Evidently, urban living did not have great appeal in this area, since Caerwent is one of the smallest *civitas* capitals, but the defences were not neglected. The first phase consisted of a ditch and bank which date, like those of most Romano-British towns, to the late second century A.D.. The stone wall was added in the third century A.D. A particular feature of the walls are the holes, one stone in size, which mark the places where scaffolding poles were fitted during construction. The north and south gates survive more or less complete, but in the fourth century A.D. both were deliberately blocked, completely in the case of the southern gate and leaving only a small opening in the case of the northern.

The defences were also strengthened at this time with polygonal bastions, of which no fewer than six survive in a good state on the south side of the town.

Within the walls you can see the footings of a typical Romano-Celtic temple with a central apsed *cella*. Surrounded by an ambulatory, the whole building is located within a walled courtyard. At the time of writing, excavations here are continuing.

Finds from Caerwent are displayed in Newport Museum. Look out for a mosaic and for casts of the Tiberius Claudius Paulinus inscription and of an altar dedicated to Mars Ocelus, presumably a native war god who has been merged with the nearest Roman equivalent.

See **Towns, Temples and Religion.**

The *civitas* capital of the Iceni is today one of a small number of Romano-British towns which are substantially devoid of later settlement. Its peaceful rural setting, however, gives no immediate hint of the troubled times which preceded its foundation.

The territory of the Iceni, which includes most of present Norfolk and Suffolk, was the homeland of Boudicca whose revolt in A.D. 60–1 almost drove the Romans prematurely from Britain. In the early years of Roman occupation, the Iceni retained a nominal independence as a client kingdom under their king, Prasutagus. Tacitus tells us that on his death, the king left half his property to his daughters and half to the Emperor Nero. Nero evidently considered this insufficient and encouraged – perhaps by Catus Decianus, the rapacious provincial procurator, an official in charge of financial matters – the army moved in to seize the whole kingdom. Acting less than prudently, they had the queen, Boudicca, flogged and raped her daughters. Fearing worse, the Iceni rebelled under Boudicca's leadership and attracted some discontented elements among the neighbouring Trinovantes. At first, Boudicca carried all before her and destroyed Colchester, London and St Albans, but eventually the governor Suetonius Paulinus, who was in north Wales at the time, managed to defeat her.

As a result of Roman retribution, it is likely that many of the Iceni's adult males were massacred or enslaved. In spite of the attempt of the succeeding procurator, Julius Classi-cianus, to heal the wounds, economic recovery in Icenian territory would have been slow, and this may explain why this tribal capital was slow to grow and never achieved the size of most of the others.

Unusually, Caister does not appear to be on the site of a fort or major native settlement, although the Iron Age hillfort of Tasburgh lies only a few miles away. Perhaps the need for a fresh start after the revolt was considered appropriate. Optimism certainly seems to have prevailed in the early years, and aerial photographs have shown a grid of streets covering a larger area than that subsequently enclosed by the defences, which is even smaller than at Caerwent. The defences are, today, represented by a ditch which is especially prominent on the east and south sides of the site, and a rampart fronted by a stone wall which can be seen on the north side, where in places it is 20-feet high, although the facing is largely missing. These defences are probably third century A.D. they had bastions added to them in the fourth century A.D. and one can still be seen a little to the north of the site of the west gate. No internal town buildings are now visible.

At the end of the Roman period, Caistor is likely to have been in one of the first areas settled by Anglo-Saxon invaders, and a little to the east of the walls, an early fifth-century A.D. cemetery was found. When an urban settlement re-emerged in this part of the country it was on a new site a few miles north which has become the city of Norwich.

See **Colchester, Towns.**

CAISTOR St EDMUND
(Venta Icenorum)
Norfolk
OS 134 TG 230035
The village is about 3 miles south of Norwich city centre. Take the A140 Ipswich Road and the first left after the junction with the B1113. On reaching Caistor, turn right at the first crossroads and look for the church on your right. It sits within the Roman defences.

Canterbury, capital of the Cantiaci *civitas*, was one of Britain's first towns, but although the site is on a strategically important crossing of the River Stour, which probably formed the first main obstacle to the conquest of this country by both Julius Caesar and the Emperor Claudius, no Roman fort has yet been identified here. The Roman town, therefore, seems to be a direct successor to a large native settlement.

Excavations suggest that the planning of the town took place over some years and the public buildings date from the 70s and 80s. One of the buildings was the theatre located at the junction of St Margaret's Street and Watling Street. The first building was probably elliptical and the *cavea* were gravel banks retained by a stone wall. It was rebuilt on the classical, semi-circular plan in the early third century A.D. Fragments of the back wall are in two premises on St Margaret's Street.

Unlike other towns in Britain, Canterbury does not seem to have been defended before the late third century A.D., when a rampart fronted by a stone wall was erected. The walls of the city today are substantially medieval, but they are in the Roman line and probably include much Roman work in their core. You should be sure to visit the Roman Quenin Gate, however, which is on the north-east part of the circuit in a car park off Broad Street. The store jambs and part of a brick arch are visible. In St Radigund's Street, a little to the west of the site of the north gate, the Roman wall appears to have been incorporated into the north wall of the church of St Mary Northgate. It probably stands to full height and there are filled-in crenellations surviving, although they are difficult to make out, which may also be Roman.

The only Roman building remains within the walls at Canterbury are housed in one of the most dismal museums the traveller is likely to find. A murky cellar in Butcher's Lane off the High Street contains the footings of a large town house but, although the mosaics are impressive it is difficult to enjoy them in these surroundings. On occasions, however, travellers may be lucky enough to see more Roman buildings emerging in excavations conducted by the Canterbury Archaeological Trust.

In the Royal Museum, shortly to be rehoused in the late medieval Poor Priests Hospital, there are two very remarkable second-century A.D. Roman cavalry men's swords to be seen.

See **Towns, Public Buildings.**

CANTERBURY
(Durovernum Cantiacorum)
Kent
OS 179 TR 150580
Canterbury is 61 miles south-east of London. Use the M2 and A2. The cathedral is justly famous, but travellers will also enjoy visiting other historic buildings here and walking around the city walls.

39

Roads

Roman roads have become legendary as one of the empire's greatest achievements. Good communications were, in fact, vital above all for the movement of troops and their supplies, but also for trade. The Britons had no roads worthy of the name, and so one of the army's first tasks after the invasion was to build a system linking the main military centres. In due course, however, London, as the economic heart of the province, became the principal road centre. All roads in the empire might lead to Rome, but in Britain they led to London.

Some of these early roads have remained major routes, and today's traveller will doubtless drive over stretches of them including, for example, Ermine Street, which ran from London to Lincoln and then on to the Humber; Watling Street, which ran from London to Wroxeter and was later extended to Chester; and the Fosse Way, which ran from Exeter to Lincoln and formed the first frontier of the Roman province in about A.D. 47. The Fosse Way also follows the pre-Roman Jurassic Way, along the great limestone ridge which ran north-west–south-east through England. Unfortunately, we do not know what the Romans called their roads, the present names are of recent origin. In addition to the trunk roads, many local roads were constructed during the Roman period as settlement patterns and trade demanded.

Tradition has it that Roman roads were straight and in favourable country, this is often so, in some cases for many miles. The military surveyors, or *agrimensores*, as representatives of the conquerors had no need to take account of the buildings or property of local people and could sweep them aside if necessary. In hilly or mountainous terrain, however, roads had to take account of contours and frequently curve and zig-zag. Rivers, marshes and dense forest might also have to be avoided and so the most striking feature of a Roman road is rather its overall straightness of alignment between major settlements, but this may hide localized changes of direction.

Once their line had been surveyed, roads were built to last. A principal consideration at all times was drainage and so, frequently, the road was laid on a slight embankment known as an *agger* which is usually all that remains visible today. The base of the road itself would be large stones, such as those which can be seen on Wheeldale Moor. The upper layers were successive deposits of stones, cobbles, or gravel rammed firmly into place and the surface would be given a gentle camber. On either side of the road, there would usually be a drainage ditch or, where it ran through a settlement, a stone gutter such as that to be seen beside the Stanegate at Corbridge. Main roads were often about 9 feet wide which would allow wheeled vehicles to pass each other; minor roads were much narrower.

Bridges were another Roman innovation, replacing hazardous fords at many river crossings. The stone bases of these bridges can still be inspected today at Chesters and Willowford on Hadrian's Wall and at Piercebridge on the River Tees.

The provincial governor was ultimately responsible for maintaining the roads in his province, but he would doubtless have devolved this onto local officials in the *civitates*. Much of the original road construction may have been done by soldiers, but maintenance was probably carried out by prisoners or forced labour. Road work was often commemorated by so-called milestones of which about 100 survive in Britain, but while they usually bear the name of the emperor in whose reign they were erected it is rare for them either to carry distances or the names of places.

The governor also had a special interest in the roads because they carried the *cursus publicus*, or imperial post, which took official messages all over the country. Messengers had road books to aid them in their travels and one of these, the *Antonine Itinerary*, which probably dates to the reign of Caracalla, has survived. It is an important source of information on Roman place names because it lists the main routes in Britain, the principal towns and forts they pass through and the distances between them. The so-called *Peutinger Table* of similar date has the same kind of information in map form. At intervals along each road, there would be places to change horses and take lodgings. These *mansiones* have been identified at a number of places in Britain, including Wall and Vindolanda and usually consist of a courtyard surrounded by small rooms with a bath house attached.

The economic effects of the road system were clearly dramatic. In particular, it enabled new markets to be found for agricultural products which stimulated farming thereby allowing a considerable accumulation of capital in the hands of landowners. What we might call the "villa economy" was heavily reliant on good communications. Industrial goods, such as pottery, could also be transported over long distances by road and this must, to a large extent, explain the development of the mass-production pottery workshops which supplied substantial areas of the country in the third and fourth centuries A.D. from places such as Water Newton and the New Forest. Since roads were so vital to farming and industry, one of the main causes of the economy's declining fortunes in the second half of the fourth century A.D. was probably a failure to maintain them, which is suggested by the lack of milestones from the period. On occasions, roads might be deliberately blocked to prevent barbarian incursions. This happened on two occasions, once only briefly and the second time permanently where the Bokerley Dyke crosses the Old Sarum to Dorchester road on the Hampshire–Dorset border.

Many roads, however, survived in use into the medieval period and can still be traced today. The traveller in search of Roman Britain will always find it satisfying, especially around major Roman towns, to look for roads either on the ground or in the modern O.S. maps. Even where they are not specifically marked, these routes may be preserved in those modern roads which are suspiciously straight, or in other landscape features. Parish boundaries, for example, were usually set out in Anglo-Saxon times and used Roman roads as convenient landmarks.

See **Ackling Dyke, Bokerley Dyke, Badbury Rings, Wheeldale.**

CARDIFF

South Glamorgan
OS 171 ST 185770

Cardiff is 155 miles west of London on the M4. The castle is at the north end of St Mary Street. The National Museum of Wales, which has Roman material on display, is close by.

Thanks to major reconstruction work at the beginning of the century, Cardiff Castle gives the traveller a unique opportunity to appreciate what a late third-century A.D. Roman fort looked like. It was, however, only the culmination of a military occupation dating from Rome's earliest interest in south Wales.

Like Brecon Gaer, Caerwent and Caerleon, Cardiff lay in the hostile territory of the Silures tribe. The first fort of about A.D. 55, therefore, represents part of the Roman policy of containment before they were finally conquered. Although it is difficult to visualize today, a map will show you that the site was chosen with the usual strategic expertise. It is on the east side of the River Taff, about $1\frac{1}{2}$ miles from the sea and covers the south-western sea approaches to Wales from the Bristol Channel.

A second, smaller, fort dates from the time that the conquest of the Silures was being completed and it was succeeded by another which was smaller again. The stone fort of about A.D. 260 indicates a new importance for the site. It is similar to some of the "Saxon Shore" forts, such as Richborough and was built to guard against seaborne invaders coming, perhaps from Ireland, up the Bristol Channel and aiming for the rich agricultural

areas of south Glamorgan and the south-west of England. The posture of the Roman army had completely changed since the days of the early forts from one of offence, when it was happy to fight the enemy in the field, to one of defence from well-fortified strong points.

Original Roman work at Cardiff is only visible to any great extent on its south side, where it occurs at the base of the wall. On the outside, it is outlined in pink stone and, on the inside, there is a stretch of 270 feet up to 16 feet high in a rather gloomy tunnel under the rampart where you will also find a mural evoking the Roman capture of the Silures. Reconstruction, however, was undertaken of the complete Roman circuit, except in the south-west quadrant. You can, therefore, see the north gate which has two storeys above a single barrel-vaulted opening and a projecting polygonal bastion on each side of the exterior. Each corner of the fort also has a bastion and others are equally spaced along the walls.

One reason for the survival of the Roman walls here was the re-use of the site for a Norman castle of which the mound, along with later medieval buildings, can still be seen. *See* **Brecon Gaer, Caerleon.**

CARMARTHEN

(Moridunum)
Dyfed
OS 159 SN 415205

Carmarthen is 27 miles north-west of Swansea by way of the M4 and A48.

The main thrust of the Roman conquest in south Wales came in the mid-70s under the governor Frontinus based on the fortress at Caerleon. The army's hold on the area was then consolidated by a network of forts and roads. It is not clear when the army reached the far south-west corner of Wales, but there is no record of stiff resistance by the local Demetae tribe comparable to that put up by the Silures to the east.

In the reign of Hadrian, many Welsh forts of the conquest period appear to have been run down due to the need for troops on his new northern frontier, and the native communities had to be trusted with a measure of self-government. It is probably at this time that the fort at Carmarthen gave way to the small *civitas* capital of Moridunum.

Although the course of the Roman defences can still be traced in the modern streets and property boundaries, there is little to see here except for the amphitheatre out-

side the town on its east side. This was constructed, like many provincial amphitheatres, by taking advantage of a natural feature. In this case, the hillslope was used for the northern *cavea*, or seating banks, and spoil from excavation into it was used for the southern *cavea*. The original arena walls have long since been removed, but today you will see a modern replacement. Although this is a simple structure, it is striking testimony to the spread of Roman civilization that such a remote place could still boast an echo of the great Colosseum in Rome itself.

While in Carmarthen, be sure to visit the museum where you can admire a silver gilt "trumpet" brooch decorated in Celtic style and the well-known gold chain from Dolaucothi. Notice also the Roman pottery which must have made a great impact on everyday life in the area since virtually none is known from pre-Roman times. *See* **Public Buildings.**

CASTELL COLLEN

Powys
OS 147 SO 055628

The nearest town to the fort is Llandrindod Wells. Take the A4081 Rhayader road and after crossing the River Ithon, look for a track on your right. Go up to a brick farmhouse where you should ask permission to see the site which is close by.

The fort at Castell Collen occupies a site similar to that of Brecon Gaer and a number of other Welsh forts, in that it overlooks a river valley, in this case the valley of the Ithon. It was founded during the Roman conquest of Wales in Frontinus's governorship and its importance in his scheme is shown by the fact that it was large enough for a 1,000-strong cavalry *ala*. The defences and internal structures were rebuilt in stone around the middle

of the second century A.D.

The rampart and ditches are still prominent, but the footings of the buildings are badly overgrown and in need of attention. In the third century A.D., the fort was reduced in size which accounts for the apparently isolated stretch of early rampart on the south side of the fort. *See* **The Army.**

The rampart and ditches at Castle Greg are so well preserved that it requires little imagination to add the timber work and so picture the fortlet's appearance in Roman times, probably during the occupation of the Antonine Wall, when it was part of the network of communications holding together a remote area of the Scottish Lowlands. Notice how strategically well-placed the fortlet is, located at almost the highest point in the locality with good views all around, but especially towards the Pentland Hills to the east. Since Castle Greg is so small, only 60 by 50 yards, it would not have been garrisoned by enough men to tackle any substantial enemy. Its main function would, therefore, have been in scouting and signalling.
See **Antonine Wall.**

The earthworks here are well camouflaged under the prolific growth of wild summer grasses.

CASTLE GREG
Midlothian
OS 65 NT 050593
The site is about 15 miles from Edinburgh. Approach it via the A70 and the B7008 to West Calder. The fortlet is just to the south of a concrete triangulation point visible on the right-hand side of the B7008 under 1 mile from the A70 intersection.

CAWTHORN

North Yorkshire
OS 100 SE 785901
The best approach is from Pickering. Take the A170 towards Kirkby Moorside and turn off in Wrelton village, then next right to Cawthorn from where you turn right again. Half a mile further on there is a rough track to the left which goes through woods to the site. At the time of writing, the National Park are planning to improve car parking and display facilities here.

In order to keep the legionaries fit and ready for campaigning, they would, like any modern army, have engaged in a variety of training exercises, one of the most important of which involved the construction of fortifications. Evidence for practice camps has been found in many parts of the country, especially near major military installations, but the best examples are in this remote area of north Yorkshire.

There are two periods of occupation here. In the first, camps A and C were occupied. The "coffin"-shaped defences of camp C are unique among Roman military works. Notice also the three entrances on the east side which have protected entrances, known as *claviculae*, which prevented a direct attack on the gateway. Camp A has much more substantial defences than C, and so it seems that the troops threw up camp C fairly quickly and then worked on building camp A.

In the second period of occupation, a rather larger body of troops appear to have enlarged camp A on its east side with an extension, i.e., camp B. Notice that the entrances are double *claviculae*. While living in camps A and B, the construction of camp

D was undertaken. You will see that the south-east corner of camp D cuts the defences of camp C, demonstrating that camp D is of a later period.

Camp D is the most elaborate of the four camps with a double-ditch system and rampart. Notice that the outer ditch is of the so-called Punic type, meaning, that it is steeper on its outer side than on the inner. An attacker arriving at the ditch would see a relatively gentle slope to jump onto but having reached the platform between the ditches, he would not only be exposed to fire from the rampart, but would find the ditch behind him much less easy to get out of than it had been to get into.

The troops who trained here are thought to have been legionaries because they evidently had *ballistae* which were mounted on platforms found during the excavations. These military catapults are not thought to have been used by auxiliary troops at the time the Cawthorn camps were constructed in the first or early second centuries A.D. The legion was presumably the Ninth based in York. *See* **York, The Army.**

CERNE GIANT

Dorset
OS 194 ST 666017
Cerne is on the A352 7 miles north of Dorchester. The best view of the giant is from a lay-by on the main road just north of the village. Cerne is a very pretty place, with the remains of an abbey and some timber-framed houses near the church.

The giant is a chalk figure, 180 feet high, cut into the side of a hill near the village of Cerne. He wields a club and on this basis has been identified as a native representation of Hercules, perhaps merged with Helith, a local Celtic fertility god. Appropriately, therefore, he is shown with his phallus erect. This organ, however, appears to be larger than it was in the eighteenth century when he also had a distinct navel. Records of the Victorian era are predictably coy about the giant's genitals

but, by the early twentieth century, his phallus seems to have been lengthened by about 6 feet by incorporation of the navel, and now measures about 30 feet. Curiously enough, this may well be the result of work under the auspices of General Pitt-Rivers, one of the greatest of Britain's early archaeologists. The giant is now in the care of the National Trust who, it is hoped, will refrain from further interference.
See **Temples and Religion.**

CHEDWORTH

Gloucestershire
OS 163 SP 052134
The villa is some 10 miles north-west of Cirencester. Take the A429, which is on the line of the Roman Fosse Way, and follow signs to Yarnworth and "Roman Villa".

The villa at Chedworth has a most attractive location, facing east at the end of a little wooded combe, or valley. It is, in fact, a classic villa site because not only is it sheltered but it has a ready water supply nearby. There is also good agricultural land in the area and there are good communications with the Fosse Way to Cirencester only a mile or so away.

Chedworth began life as a fairly modest Romanized farm, at first having three discrete buildings on terraces into the sloping ground. In about A.D. 300, however, these buildings were unified into a most luxurious establishment enclosing a garden court on three sides, with a wall running along the fourth. The owner of this villa clearly belonged in the upper echelons of local society and the basis of his wealth was probably trading in farm products with Cirencester, which also seems to have prospered in this period.

Mosaics are a good indicator of wealth and in the *triclinium* or dining room, in the west wing there is a pavement of the local Cor-

inium (Cirencester) school. A geometric design can be seen in the room where the diners sat and on the anteroom floor, which would have been unencumbered by furniture, there is a depiction of the god Bacchus and the four seasons. Notice that the personification of winter is wearing a cloak thought to be characteristically British and known as a *birrus Britannicus*. After the *triclinium*, you come to one of the villa's bath suites which, in this case, offered steamy heat like that found in a Turkish bath. The other bath suite, in the north wing, was of the dry heat or sauna type.

East of the northern baths is a room with a polygonal apse. Apses are a common feature of high-quality Roman villas and town houses. They may have been used as shrines or for the accommodation of the couches on which good Romans reclined to dine. Next to this room is one which had a hypocaust heating system, the floor having been supported on a forest of stone pillars. At the far end of the north wing are five rooms which belong to the final alterations at Chedworth which were as late as the 370s.

In the north-west corner of the site, there is a building known as the Nymphaeum. This is where the spring rises and there was at one time a shrine here to its presiding deity, presumably a water nymph. In the fourth century A.D., however, the villa inhabitants were evidently Christian and a chi-rho symbol, the first letters of Christ's name in Greek, were carved into the wall of the Nymphaeum and onto other stones from the villa.

Chedworth is not only one of the most informative villa sites in Britain, but it also illustrates some of the more encouraging developments in the display of historic sites, as well as some of the problems. There is a good audio-visual introduction to the site in the National Trust visitor reception centre, and an excellent guidebook. On the other hand, many rooms are enclosed by rather unprepossessing "chalets", and the surviving walls have dreadful little roofs on them. There must be some better way of preservation. The museum contains some interesting sculpture, including two pleasantly crude carvings of a native god, Mars Lenus, but the finds are poorly displayed. It is to be hoped that the National Trust will change this soon.

See **Cirencester, Villas.**

The Roman army chose the site of Chester for a fort in about A.D. 78 or 79. From here they could guard a strategic crossing of the River Dee and keep an eye on both the recently pacified Ordovices of north Wales, and the Brigantes of northern England. Construcion was undertaken by the Second Legion, known as Adiutrix (auxiliary) Pia Fidelis (loyal and faithful), sent from Lincoln for the purpose. It was not, however, to form the permanent garrison here, as it was withdrawn from Britain by A.D. 87 to meet a crisis on the Rhine frontier. As a result of the loss of a legion, the army in Britain had to withdraw from Scotland to the Tyne–Solway frontier. Among the returning troops was the Twentieth Legion which, after a short stay in its base at Wroxeter, was moved forward to garrison Chester in the early 90s. From this time on, Chester, along with Caerleon and York, was to be one of the three permanent legionary bases in Britain.

The best place to begin your visit to Roman Chester is the Grosvenor Museum, where you will see a model of the fortress and of various buildings associated with it. The museum also has one of the finest collections of Roman sculpture in Britain. Look out for tombstones of soldiers from both the Second and Twentieth Legions, and of civilians such as Curatia Dionysia, who is shown reclining in true Roman manner on a couch with a goblet in her right hand, possibly symbolizing a funeral meal.

You should then take a walk around the justly famous walls of Chester which are substantially Roman on the east and north sides of the circuit. The first fortress defences consisted of a ditch and rampart with a timber palisade and towers. In the early second century A.D., during the reign of the Emperor Trajan, Roman military dispositions were made permanent in Britain, and so reconstruction of buildings and defences in stone was undertaken at all three legionary fortresses. The work at Chester was probably left incomplete, however, when the legion was sent north to tackle the erection of Hadrian's Wall. Full regarrisoning of the fortress was not achieved until after the final retreat from Scotland in the 160s.

In the late second century A.D., a splendid new fortress wall was built, consisting of a chamfered plinth at the base, thirteen courses of large sandstone blocks and a decorative cornice surmounted by a parapet which may have been crenellated. The best places to see the Roman work, which often lacks only the parapet, are behind No. 12, St John's Street; near the Cathedral in Mercia Square, either side of Kaleyard Gate; and along the north side of the circuit overlooking the canal. It was in repairs to this northern stretch late in the last century that the majority of the inscribed stones in the museum were found. They had been used in a thickening of the upper part of the wall in the late third or early fourth centuries A.D., when it became free standing due to a reduction in the height of the rampart. This may have been the work of Constantius Chlorus, who restored Britain's defences after the revolt of Carausius and Allectus. Free-standing walls were part of the new ideas on military architecture at the time.

Within the fortress, there are a few places where pieces of Roman building work either remain *in situ* or have been marked out in modern materials, but none of them are spectacular. What is spectacular, however, is the amphitheatre located to the south-east of the fortress. It was the largest in Roman Britain and the northern half has been completely excavated. It was initially constructed in timber but was soon rebuilt in stone. The massive buttressed outside walls originally stood 40 feet high. The main entrance into the arena has a Nemeseum on one side – a shrine to Nemesis, Goddess of Vengeance, at whose altar the gladiator might well have contemplated his uncertain fate.

See **Caerleon, Caernafon, York, The Army, Emperors in Britain, Public Buildings.**

CHESTER
(Deva)
Cheshire
OS 117 SJ 405665
Chester is 188 miles north-west of London by way of the M6 and 35 miles south-west of Manchester. While in the city, be sure to visit the cathedral and other historic buildings, as well as the Roman remains.

Emperors in Britain
Nobles and Savages?

Although Britannia was a far-flung part of the empire and remained something of a cultural backwater throughout the Roman era, it frequently found itself at the centre of imperial politics. For 350 years, strenuous efforts were made in its defence. Three legions were permanently stationed here, which incidentally gave governors great potential and, on occasions, actual influence in the choice of emperor, and the most elaborate frontier system in the Roman world lay between the Tyne and the Solway. Even in the dark days of the later fourth century A.D., there is evidence for major defensive works on urban and military sites.

The reason for imperial concern was probably partly economic – Britain was, in a way, the "bread basket of the west" – partly symbolic. Because Britain was remote and mysterious, its conquest was hailed as a great event and its retention remained a matter of particular pride. Indeed, its very remoteness and the unsophisticated nature of its people seems to have taken hold of the imagination of the Romans and have been used by some to expose the decadence and corruption of Rome itself. As Juvenal puts it:

> Though our armies have advanced
> To Ireland, though the Orkneys are ours, and northern Britain
> With its short clear nights, these conquered tribes abhor
> The vices that flourish in their conqueror's capital.

The first Roman leader to risk the dreaded ocean and go beyond, as it was thought, the end of the world was Julius Caesar in two brief missions of a basically punitive nature. The Emperor Augustus contemplated an invasion, as did the mad Caligula, who on receiving Adminius, son of King Cunobelin, even claimed that the whole island had submitted to him. The first emperor to visit Britain, however, was Claudius who formally took the surrender of eleven British tribes at Colchester. Although Suetonius remarks "Claudius's sole campaign was of no great importance", Britain provided him with a much-needed military success to secure his grip on power, and he obviously made the most of it for Suetonius adds: "His triumph was a very splendid one."

Commanding one of the legions which undertook the conquest, there was another future emperor, Vespasian, who campaigned vigorously in the south-west. Although Vespasian never returned to Britain, he was responsible for the appointment of Gnaeus Julius Agricola to the governorship – the man whose career was immortalized by his son-in-law, Tacitus. In *The Agricola*, Tacitus also develops the theme of the noble savage putting, for example, a fine speech on liberty into the mouth of Calgacus, leader of the Caledonians, before the battle of Mons Graupius. The words reflect the views of a politician of the Roman republic to which many educated men of Tacitus's time looked back to as to a golden age – not surprisingly, in view of the excesses of the reign of Domitian.

The next emperor to visit Britain, Hadrian, like Trajan before him, was a provincial from Spain and so, perhaps, able to distance himself a little from the intrigues and depravity of Rome itself. His reign also signals something of a new mood in imperial affairs: the unquestioned aim of world conquest was effectively abandoned and the emperor spent much of his reign travelling to ensure that the empire's frontiers were secure. Apart from a brief reference by his biographer to a "wall to divide Rome from the Barbarians", we know few details of his stay in Britain, although Hadrian's preoccupations are evident from the minting of commemorative coins showing Britannia carrying a shield and gazing out watchfully over the northern hills. One cannot help wondering, however, how much time he spent in the fortress at York, or even perhaps in a draughty tent near Carlisle or Vindolanda, poring over maps and plans of the monument which has assured him immortality.

Britain had to wait over 80 years for another imperial visitor and Septimius Severus's arrival, ostensibly to campaign north of Hadrian's Wall, may again be connected with the notion of Britain as a home of savage nobility, if not of noble savages, since there seems little doubt that he wished to get his quarrelling sons, Geta and Caracalla, away from the flesh pots and intrigue of Rome. In the event, the campaigns of Severus, who at 60 was past his prime, were inconclusive and, since he was a north African, the climate can hardly have suited him. Indeed, it may have helped to kill him in A.D. 211 when he became the first of two emperors to die in York. Caracalla and Geta swiftly left Britain to join the power struggle in Rome. Severus himself was cremated with much ceremony and his ashes were taken to Rome in an urn of purple stone. There is still an area of York known as the Severus Hills.

As a footnote to Severus's visit, Cassius Dio relates an amusing incident which again casts light on the way moral standards might differ between Britain and Rome, not necessarily to the latter's advantage. The Empress Julia Domna, on meeting the wife of a Caledonian named Argentocoxus, referred to the tribal practice of the women having "free intercourse with men" to which the woman replied: "We fulfil nature's demands much better than you Roman women: we openly associate with the best men, you commit adultery with the worst in secret."

In the political turmoil of the third century A.D., emperors came and went with rapidity and Britain even ceased to be ruled from Rome for a while when it became part of the "Gallic Empire" from A.D. 260 to A.D. 274 and then again in A.D. 286 when Britain, along with parts of northern Gaul, gained independence as an *insulum imperiae*, or island empire. The usurper, Carausius, gets a uniformly bad press from legitimate imperial sources which attributed his seizure of power to a desire to cover up the embezzlement of captured spoils. Oddly enough,

Carausius may have been something of a noble savage, in that we know he was from a humble background in Menapia, now Belgium, and had risen to command of the channel fleet from the rank of steersman. He was, however, an effective naval commander and his restoration of the coinage by increasing its silver content suggests an able administrator. Carausius's luck began to run out when the new junior emperor, or Caesar, in the west, Constantius Chlorus, managed to capture Boulogne. Carausius was then murdered by his minister, Allectus, who proved to be no war-leader.

Constantius is again recorded visiting Britain as senior emperor, or Augustus, in the west in A.D. 305, presumably to inspect the new defence works he had initiated, especially on Hadrian's Wall. The existence of junior and senior emperors in the eastern and western halves of the empire was the result of the new governmental system known as the Tetrarchy, established by the Emperor Diocletian in an attempt to lift the burden of administration from a single leader and to make the succession more orderly. The system was further secured by family ties and, around the time Constantius became Caesar in the west, he divorced his Christian wife, Helena, who was later canonized, to marry the daughter of the Augustus of the time, Maximian. On his campaigns in Britain, however, Constantius was accompanied by his son by Helena, Constantine, and on his death in York in July A.D. 306, Constantine was instantly acclaimed Augustus by the troops. The Tetrarchy was dead, although it took Constantine until A.D. 318 to become sole emperor.

We cannot tell if Constantine thought of York with special affection but the great, rebuilt south-west front to the fortress surely bears the stamp of a man who marked his reign with numerous projects of awesome architectural magnificence. On some of his coins, Constantine identifies himself as the "unconquered sun" and during his reign the imperial *numen* certainly shone on Britain as it underwent a marked economic revival.

Following the death of Constantine, the last legitimate emperor to visit these shores was his son, Constans, in A.D. 343, after which Britain became once more a base for usurpers seeking the imperial crown. Among them was Magnentius in A.D. 350, a general whose mother may have been British; Magnus Maximus, the Macsen Wledig of Welsh legend, who was probably the *dux Britanniarum*, or commander of the northern frontier garrison; and finally Constantine III whose attempt to seize power, which failed in A.D. 411, must have removed most of the remaining Roman soldiers from Britain.

See **Caernafon, Colchester, Richborough, York, Hadrian's Wall.**

The medieval walls of Chichester follow the course of their Roman predecessors which were built, perhaps, in the mid-third century A.D. and North, South, East and West Streets lie roughly over the main streets of the Roman town. The main reason why the traveller in search of Roman Britain should visit Chichester, however, is an inscription to be seen under the portico of the Assembly Rooms. It is a dedication by a guild of craftsmen to Neptune and Minerva on behalf of a man named Tiberius Claudius Cogidubnus, who is referred to as "Great King in Britain". This is important because it indicates that the area around Chichester was, in the early years of Roman rule, a client kingdom rather than a fully integrated part of the province.

Cogidubnus very probably retained his independence because he was actively pro-Roman, an attribute confirmed by Tacitus in the *Agricola*, where he states that Cogidubnus "maintained his unswerving loyalty right down to our own times", but then adds cynically that he is "an example of the long-established Roman custom of employing even kings to make others slaves". The extent of Cogidubnus's realm is uncertain, but it may have included much of Sussex, Hampshire, Surrey and Berkshire with centres both at Chichester and Silchester. As a special mark of favour, the Romans may also have constructed the Fishbourne palace for Cogidubnus's private use.
See **Fishbourne, Silchester.**

CHICHESTER
(Noviomagus Regnensium)
West Sussex
OS 197 SU 861048
Chichester is 66 miles south-west of London and 18 miles east of Portsmouth. It is an attractive city with many good Georgian buildings and a fine cathedral.

Cirencester, Corinium Dobunnorum, lay in one of the most prosperous parts of Roman Britain, and so it is not surprising that it grew to become one of the largest towns. Evidence for its importance is provided by an inscription which suggests that Corinium was the capital of Britannia Prima, one of the four provinces into which Britain was divided in the early fourth century A.D. Roman Cirencester's origins, however, lay in a fort established here within the first year or so of the invasion, which was succeeded by a more permanent establishment in around A.D. 49. It would have guarded the point where the River Churn was crossed by the Fosse Way, boundary of the British province in the early years of the conquest. Initially, the garrison was a cavalry regiment of Thracians from Greece, and there is a fine tombstone of Sextus Valerius Genialis one of their troopers, in the Corinium Museum.

In the late Iron Age the local tribe, known as the Dobunni, had a major centre in an enclosure at Bagendon, 2 miles north of Cirencester. Once the area was securely under Roman rule, they were probably happy to transfer their allegiance to the *civitas* capital founded on the site of the fort in the mid-70s. Nothing can be seen of the town's buildings today, but it is known that the forum, which formed the civic centre, lay a little to the south-east of the present centre of Cirencester on a site between the Avenue and Lewis Lane.

The defences follow a similar pattern to that observed in many Romano-British towns with a ditch and earthen rampart constructed in the late second century, A.D., but with gates and interval towers in stone. At some stage in the first half of the third century A.D., a stone wall was added to the front of the rampart and in the fourth century A.D. Cirencester was one of the towns to have projecting bastions added to the walls, possibly as a result of Count Theodosius's work in the late 360s. A stretch of wall still survives today on the north-east side of the circuit, just off the London Road, where you can also see the rampart, one of the original stone towers and two of the projecting bastions.

Apart from the walls, the most impressive Roman structure surviving at Cirencester today is the amphitheatre to be found on the south-west side of the town in an area now known as the Querns. This was originally the site of a quarry and the *cavea* around the amphitheatre's arena were built up from quarry waste. You can see the two main arena entrances, but the rest is grassed over. Excavations have shown, however, that there were some thirty rows of seats and it has been calculated that about 6,000 people could have been accommodated here.

The prosperity of the citizenry is most graphically demonstrated by the large number of mosaic pavements found in Cirencester. The earliest are second century A.D., but the majority date from the fourth century A.D., when there appears to have been a school of mosaicists, known as the Corinium school, operating in the area. One of their favourite themes was Orpheus who, with his lyre, charmed the beasts and moved trees and rocks. An Orpheus pavement from Cirencester can be seen in the museum, but the most famous, perhaps, is that at Woodchester Villa nearby, although it is only displayed on rare occasions. Another fine mosaic in the museum depicts the four seasons along with two mythological scenes: one of Silenus on a donkey and one of Actaeon being torn to pieces by his dogs – punishment for spying on Diana bathing.

Besides the mosaics, the Corinium Museum has many other important Roman finds, including the mysterious Christian acrostic or word square which loses the word "paternoster" and the alpha and omega in the apparently innocent ROTAS OPERA TENET AREPO SATOR, which is translated as "Arepo the sower holds the wheels by his effort."
See **Towns.**

CIRENCESTER
(Corinium Dubunnorum)
Gloucestershire
OS 163 SP 025015
Cirencester is 95 miles west-north-west of London. Take the M4 to Junction 15, and then the A419. While in the town, be sure to visit the parish church, the size of which reflects medieval prosperity derived from the wool trade.

COLCHESTER

(Camulodunum)

Essex

OS 168 TL 994254

Colchester is 63 miles north-east of London on the A12.

As you stroll in the calm of Colchester's Castle Park, try to imagine the scene here in A.D. 60 when, according to Tacitus, the citizens of the infant Roman colony made their desperate last stand against the incensed hordes of Queen Boudicca. Fighting hand to hand on the steps of the Temple of Claudius, where the Norman Castle now stands, the town burnt fiercely around them and stragglers, were mercilessly put to death.

Quite apart from this awful climax, however, Colchester is one of the most important and exciting sites for the early history of the Romans in Britain. Immediately before the invasion it had been the capital of the Catuvellauni, the pre-eminent tribe in south-east England. Their settlement, located a little to the south-west of the present town centre, covered a large area guarded by a complex system of man-made banks and ditches known as dykes. Three dykes – on the Lexden dyke, the Lexden triple dyke and Gryme's dyke – are still clearly visible today on the west side of the town, although archaeological work suggests that the last two were probably constructed in the early Roman period.

The greatest king of the Catuvellauni was Cunobelin who died in about A.D. 40. He has passed into literature as Shakespeare's Cymbeline, and the so-called Lexden tumulus to be found in a garden in Fitzwalter Avenue may mark his tomb. A number of fine grave goods were found in it, including a medallion of the Emperor Augustus. The aristocracy of the Britons here may have been politically anti-Roman, but they were happy to embrace Roman taste. Another burial mound of this period which is rather better preserved is the Mount, in nearby Marlowe Way.

The death of Cunobelin resulted in the succession of his two anti-Roman sons, Caratacus and Togodumnus. A third son, Adminius, took a different view and fled to Rome, perhaps thereby providing a pretext for the Roman invasion. The formal submission of Britain was taken at Colchester by the Emperor Claudius who thus recognized the dominance that the Catuvellauni had achieved in native affairs. A fortress of the Twentieth Legion was then built here. There is nothing of this to be seen, but extensive excavations have shown that the Lion Walk and Culver Street shopping malls lie at the heart of it. In the museum, be sure to see the tombstone of Marcus Favonius Facilis, a centurion of the Twentieth Legion, who proudly holds the vine staff, his symbol of office.

In A.D. 49 the legion moved on and the Colonia Claudia Victricensis was founded for legionary veterans on the same site. It was the first of a number of Roman towns, including Exeter, Gloucester and Lincoln, to develop out of fortresses and even to reuse some of their streets and buildings. The defences at Colchester were, however, filled in – a fatal mistake for which the colonists were to pay dearly. One reason for infilling was to allow the town to expand eastwards and here the public buildings were erected. Chief among them was the temple of the deified Emperor Claudius. Amazingly enough, its foundation still survive. They are known as the Castle Vaults, although this is a misnomer. When the temple was built, a rectangular trench and two cross trenches were dug into the ground. Their sides were shored with timber and they were then filled with concrete to make a base for the superstructure. In modern times the earth between the concrete filled trenches has been dug out to give the appearance of vaults. The temple itself would have been a classical-style building similar to that at Bath with steps leading up to a podium on which the shrine would have been approached by a tetrasytle (four-columned) entrance surmounted by a pediment, no doubt bearing impressive relief carvings.

Another early public building was the theatre of a classic semi-circular form. Part of the curving outer wall can be seen in a small display building in Maidenburgh Street, and in the footings of St Helen's Chapel further along the street.

The new colony was seen by the native population, again to quote Tacitus, as the "citadel of everlasting oppression", and the arrogance of the Roman citizens in seizing land and property may have done much to fuel discontent. In excavations, archaeological evidence for Boudicca's revolt is frequently found as a thick burnt layer, but in the museum look out for the tombstone of cavalryman, Longinus Sdapeze. Notice that his face has been mutilated, probably by the rebels, while that of the cowering native below him is untouched.

Once the Romans had regained control a free-standing triumphal arch was erected over the main entry to the town on its west side. In the early second century A.D., this was incorporated into what is now known as the Balkerne Gate, built as part of the town walls. The excavation of the Gate, one of the best surviving Roman gates in all Britain, was hampered by the appropriately named "Hole in the Wall" pub, which sits over a good part of it, but as a result of the work of Sir Mortimer Wheeler and, more recently, by the Colchester Archaeological Trust, and the principal features may be inspected by the visitor.

The walls of Colchester are the first free standing town walls in Britain and they survive, if much repaired, over most of their original circuit of 3,007 yards in places up to 18 feet high. The best places to see them are either side of the Balkerne Gate. On the north side of the walled area in the Castle Park is the so-called Duncan Gate. It was single portalled; part of the arch over the opening, having fallen, was found behind and has been left in place.

See **Caistor St Edmund, Native Background, The Army, Emperors in Britain, Towns, Public Buildings, Temples and Religion.**

If the Romans were initially unwilling to advance into Britain's more mountainous areas, they were soon constrained to do so in order not only to quell their hostile inhabitants, but also to seize their mineral wealth. One of the minerals – listed by the Roman geographer Strabo, writing in the early first century A.D., as an export from Britain – was gold.

In pre-Roman and Roman times most British gold probably came from the mines at Dolaucothi, but Roman engineers with their superior technological expertise would have greatly increased the scale of operations. One of their innovations was a sophisticated drainage system used in deep shafts, and part of a wheel from the equipment was found in more modern mining.

DOLAUCOTHI
Dyfed
OS 146 SN 664394
The site of the mines lies a little to the south-east of the hamlet of Pumsaint, which is on the A482 some 8 miles south-east of Lampeter. Dolaucothi is in the care of the National Trust and well signposted from the main road.

The site today has an attractive sylvan setting and no longer echoes to the sounds of men at work. Distinguishing Roman from more modern shafts is not easy, but most of the openings are probably Roman in origin. After walking up past the mines, you eventually come to a grassy field in which there is a shallow depression cut into the hilly slope. This is the site of a reservoir at the end of an aqueduct, which supplied water both for breaking up the gold-bearing rock and for panning to separate gold from dross.

Most of Dolaucothi's gold probably went to the imperial mints, but a few gold objects have been found locally, including a chain with wheel pendant to be seen in Carmarthen Museum.

Thanks to excellent organisation, a visit to Dolaucothi will be an enjoyable and informative affair, with interest both above and below ground.

DORCHESTER

(Durnovaria)
Dorset
OS 194 SY 690900
*Dorchester is 121 miles south-west
of London. Take the M3 to
Southampton and then follow the
M27, A31 and A35.*

*The grassy slopes of Maumbury Rings
are to be found just beyond
Dorchester Station, off the A354 to
Weymouth; and attract sun-seekers as
well as those in search of ancient sites.*

In Roman times, the pleasant market town of Dorchester, Thomas Hardy's Casterbridge, was capital of the *civitas* of the Durotriges. Immediately after the conquest there may have been a fort here guarding the crossing of the River Frome by the road to Exeter and keeping an eye on the local population, which had been recently humiliated by the storming of nearby Maiden Castle. By the 70s or 80s, however, men such as Carinus – whose tombstone, now in Fordington Church, proudly proclaims him to be a Roman citizen – were happy to become inhabitants of the new town.

In the late second century A.D. Dorchester, like so many Romano-British towns, acquired defences: first a ditch and earthen rampart and, in the late third century A.D., a stone wall. The rampart still accounts for the height of the pavement alongside the Grove in the north-west part of the town, and a sad fragment of wall survives just south of the roundabout at the top of the High Street.

The only Roman building remains are of a house in Colliton Park behind the council offices. It was constructed in the fourth century A.D. when Dorchester, along with villas in the surrounding countryside, were enjoying a period of great prosperity. All the rooms in the western range had mosaics of the local Dorchester school, although only one can be seen *in situ*. Travellers may be surprised to learn that the Romans had mastered the art

of glazing windows, and an unusual feature of the Dorchester house is a window embrasure. After the Roman era glazing did not become common again until the seventeenth century.

The other Roman monument not to be missed in Dorchester is the amphitheatre known as Maumbury Rings, a little to the south of the town centre. It was originally a Neolithic henge monument adapted in the Roman period by reusing the banks for seating and lowering the centre to form the arena. Although its life as a civic amenity seems, for some reason, to have been short, the Rings were used for defence in the Civil War and for gun emplacements in the Second World War.

The Roman finds in the museum are displayed in an attractive new gallery which has adopted as its theme the importance of conserving ancient sites and monuments. Notice the products of the local Kimmeridge shale industry. Shale is a soft stone, not unlike coal, which can be easily worked into small objects, such as spindle whorls, or larger decorative and functional items such as the fine table leg on display here. The relief of a man on horseback from nearby Witcombe is also of interest and, finally, there are more mosaics of the Dorchester school set in the ground floor of the museum.

See **Towns.**

Towns
The Seeds of Civilization

The first-century A.D. mosaic from Fishbourne, showing a stylized street grid surrounded by a crenellated wall with gates, reminds us that Roman civilization was essentially an urban civilization. The political and social structure of the Mediterranean world was based on communities which not only had densely built-up commercial settlements at their heart, but which had a well-developed ability to govern and tax themselves under imperial supervision.

The success of Romanization in Britain depended on integrating the country into a town-based governmental system, but at the time of the conquest there was nowhere which would have merited designation as a town, the population for the most part living in scattered rural settlements. Some of the more important tribal centres may have acquired what we might call "urban functions" as centres of government, industry and trade, but they did not have a distinct legal status or house an appreciable concentration of population. We should not underestimate, therefore, the problems Agricola faced when we hear that "his object was to accustom them [the Britons] to a life of peace and quiet by the provision of amenities. He, therefore, gave private encouragement and official assistance to the building of temples, public squares and good houses".

Colchester can justifiably claim to be Britain's first town. As the principal centre of the Catuvellauni, it had been important to establish a military presence there after the invasion, but when the army moved on the fortress site was used for a *colonia*. *Coloniae* occupied the highest rank of Roman chartered towns and in early imperial times they were created in the provinces by the settlement of legionary veterans who were then counted on both to spread the virtues of Roman civilization and to act as an army reserve. Two further *coloniae* were created in Britain at the end of the first century A.D. on the site of fortresses at Gloucester and Lincoln. York was elevated to colonial status in the early third century A.D. in recognition of its size and prosperity.

Another early town foundation was at St Albans which, according to Tacitus, was a *municipium* – another form of chartered town. The significance of both *coloniae* and *municipia* is that their inhabitants included Roman citizens and, therefore, had legal privileges in Roman law not accorded to the rest of the population. After the reign of Caracalla (A.D. 211–17), however, when all free people of the empire became citizens, the distinction mattered less.

The government of a chartered town was, to a large extent, modelled on that of Rome itself. It was ruled by an *ordo* of, nominally, 100 *decurions*, or councillors, who had to own a certain amount of property and be local residents. The *ordo* was run by a pair of magistrates who were rotated annually. The chief responsibilities of the *ordo* were to adminster justice, collect taxes and undertake public works, for which, to a large extent, they were required to pay out of their own pockets.

Outside the chartered towns, the inhabitants of Britain were referred to as *peregrini*, or non-citizens, and were organized into local government areas known as *civitates* largely based on pre-existing chiefdom boundaries. Within the *civitas*, people nominally had the same legal status wherever they lived, although government was based in the *civitas* capital – a town founded by deliberate official planning. This would be the seat of the *ordo*. An interesting insight into local government practice comes from the inscription from Caerwent which refers to a decree of the *res publica* (public body) of the *civitas* of the Silures, meaning the people as a whole, rather than simply the town of Venta Silurum.

The first *civitas* capitals were, in addition to the *municipium* at St Albans, at Canterbury and Chelmsford. More were added as the southern part of Britain was pacified. When Hadrian needed extra troops to garrison his northern frontier, further areas had to be allowed self-government and new *civitates* were created with capitals at places such as Aldborough and Caerwent.

Although none of the British towns were large by the standards of some great Mediterranean cities, a population of about 5,000 being the usual maximum, all Roman towns shared a number of characteristics which could be recognized anywhere in the empire. They would have a regular grid of metalled streets with proper drains; the spaces between the streets were known as *insulae*. The forum would be at the centre, along with other public buildings and there would be shops on the main street frontages. Somewhere on the outskirts there might be an amphitheatre and, adjacent to roads radiating from the town, were the cemeteries.

Initially, defences were by no means a universal component of town layout and one reason for Boudicca's success was that Colchester and London were undefended. Later first-century A.D. towns which grew out of fortresses retained their defences, three of the early *civitas* capitals – Winchester, Silchester and Chichester – had a bank and ditch, and Colchester acquired a wall in the early second century A.D., but otherwise the great move to defend towns came in the later second century. In general terms, the first phase took the form of a ditch and earthen rampart to which a stone wall was added sometime in the third century A.D.. These walls are often the most prominent Roman structures remaining in Britain's towns today, largely because their medieval walls usually followed the same line and reused much of the Roman masonry.

The reason for the erection of the defences is not clear, but since it would have required official approval at the highest level, they are, perhaps, best considered as a response to some political event. This could have been the incursions recorded by Cassius Dio in the mid-180s or the withdrawal of Britain's garrison by Clodius Albinus. Further work in the third century A.D. may be connected with a general deterioration of the political situation.

Political instability and the resulting disruption of trade seems to have caused most towns to stagnate in the third century A.D. both in terms of population and prosperity, but the return to strong government in the late third and early fourth centuries A.D. temporarily created conditions for renewed growth and for new towns such as Water Newton with its extensive industrial activities. After about A.D. 350, however, serious changes in the urban order took place. Although occupation continued, and in St Albans new mosaics were even laid, grass started to grow in the streets, public buildings deteriorated and, perhaps most significant, burials were made within settled areas. Terminal decline was just around the corner.

The enhancement of urban defences with bastions in the late fourth century A.D. may best be seen as the creation of fortified strong points in which not only the citizens, but also the population of the surrounding areas could seek protection at times of crisis. Recognizable urban life can hardly have existed, however, in A.D. 410, when the famous letter telling the cities of Britain to look to their own defence arrived from the Emperor Honorius, thereby effectively ending Roman rule in this country.

See **Colchester, St Albans, Silchester, Public Buildings, Bath Houses.**

A sculptured fragment from Corstopitum.

DOVER
(Dubris)
Kent
OS 179 TR 325415
Dover is 77 miles south-east of London via the M2 and A2.

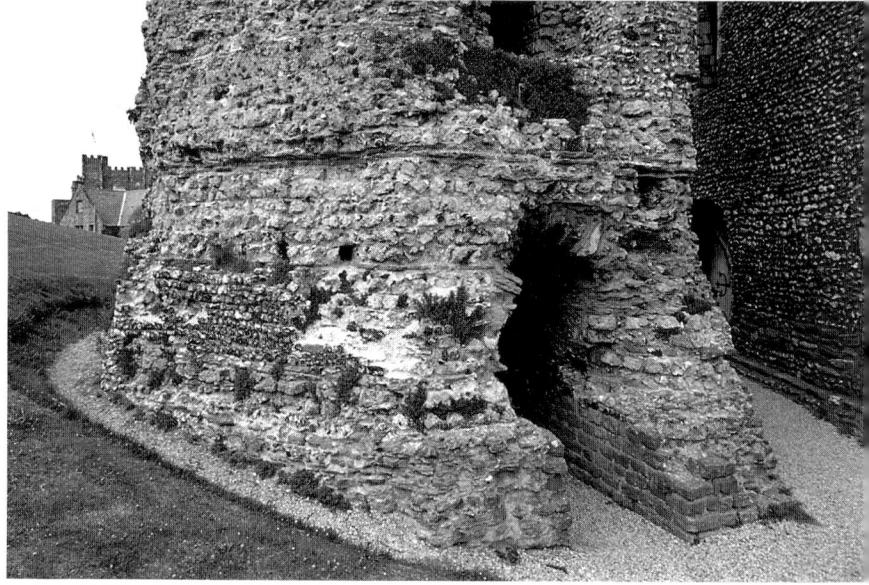

The Roman base of the Pharos shares its cliff-top site with Dover Castle.

Anyone who has travelled across the Channel from France will be familiar with the famous White Cliffs of Dover. As well as a welcome, however, the great chalk precipices have also presented something of an obstacle over the centuries to would-be invaders. Julius Caesar cannot have been the first and was certainly not the last leader to confront this problem. In *De bello Gallico*, he records his impressions of our shores as follows:

> Caesar himself reached Britain with the first ships about nine o'clock in the morning, and saw the enemy's forces posted on all the hills. The lie of the land at this point was such that javelins could be hurled from the cliffs right onto the narrow beach enclosed between them and the sea. Caesar thought this a quite unsuitable place for landing.

In the event, he went around the coast of Kent and landed somewhere in the Deal area.

There is a gap in the cliffs, however, at a point where the River Dour flows into the sea and, since the shortest sea crossing to France is from this point, it was an obvious site for a Roman harbour and base of the Classis Britannica, or British Fleet. We do not usually think of the Romans as a maritime people but ships had an important role to play in military operations, especially on an island like Britain. They would have supported the army in the invasion and in subsequent campaigns, transporting stones and bulky equipment and patrolling and exploring the coast.

We know of the existence of the Classis Britannica, both from inscriptions such as that found at Benwell and from large numbers of tiles stamped "CLBR" which were made in its official workshops. The distribu-

tion of these tiles shows that the fleet's centre of operations was around the coast of south-east Britain and in the Channel with two major bases at Dover and Boulogne. The Classis Britannica fort at Dover has recently been discovered. It was constructed in about A.D. 130 and was occupied until perhaps the mid-third century A.D.

In the later third century A.D. a new fort was built as part of the "Saxon Shore" defensive system along the south and east coast of Britain where barbarian pirates roamed at will. The crisis was apparently so serious that opulent town houses were swept away to make room for the fort. At one point, its wall was found cutting through an earlier house and the rampart behind the wall had completely buried, and thus preserved, several rooms. These can now be seen in the Painted House Museum which has the most extensive display of *in situ* painted wall plaster anywhere in Britain.

Another important feature of the Roman harbour was a pair of lighthouses sited on the cliffs either side of the river estuary. The western lighthouse has been largely demolished, but the eastern one, modelled on the great third-century B.C. *pharos* in Alexandria and now in the grounds of Dover Castle, remains one of the most substantial Roman buildings surviving in Britain today. It is now 62 feet high, although the upper 19 feet are medieval, but originally it was probably some 80 feet high and would have resembled an inverted telescope with each successive floor set back from the one below. Battered by the weather of centuries it may be, but one can still picture its great beacon reassuring sailors and passengers on a sea crossing which was far more hazardous than in these days of "roll-on, roll-off" ferries and hovercraft.

See **Burgh Castle, Lympne, Richborough.**

We know from Suetonius, that the Second Augustan Legion under its commander, the future Emperor Vespasian, encountered stiff resistance in the territory of the Durotriges centred on what is now Dorset. They appear to have had an easier ride, however, when they met the Dumnonii of Devon and Cornwall. We do not know if Vespasian himself established the legionary fortress at Exeter in about A.D. 55, but his campaigns in the south-west earned him high honour in Rome and set him on his way to the imperial crown.

The fortress lay on a spur of land overlooking the River Exe, a name derived from the first element in the towns Romano-British name, "Isca". Military occupation lasted until about A.D. 75 when the site was taken over for the local *civitas* capital, even to the extent of reuse of the defences, streets and buildings, including the legionary bath house which was converted into the forum. Substantial remains of this building were found in excavations on the Cathedral Green, but they have unfortunately been reburied awaiting resources for proper public display.

Roman Exeter grew rapidly and the defences constructed in the late second century A.D. enclosed a much larger area than the fortress. The walls were built largely out of trap, a local purple-grey volcanic stone which outcrops in Rougemont, where the castle now stands. The Roman circuit was retained in Saxon and medieval times and until recently most of the inhabitants of Exeter still lived within it. You can still see original Roman work surviving up to 12 feet high to the south-west of the south gate by a path leading to the historic seventeenth-century Custom house.
See **Towns.**

EXETER
(Isca Dumnoniorum)
Devon
OS 192 SX 919925
Exeter is 170 miles south-west of London. Take the M3 to Junction 8 (Popham) and then the A303. While in the city, be sure to visit the cathedral and castle, as well as the walls.

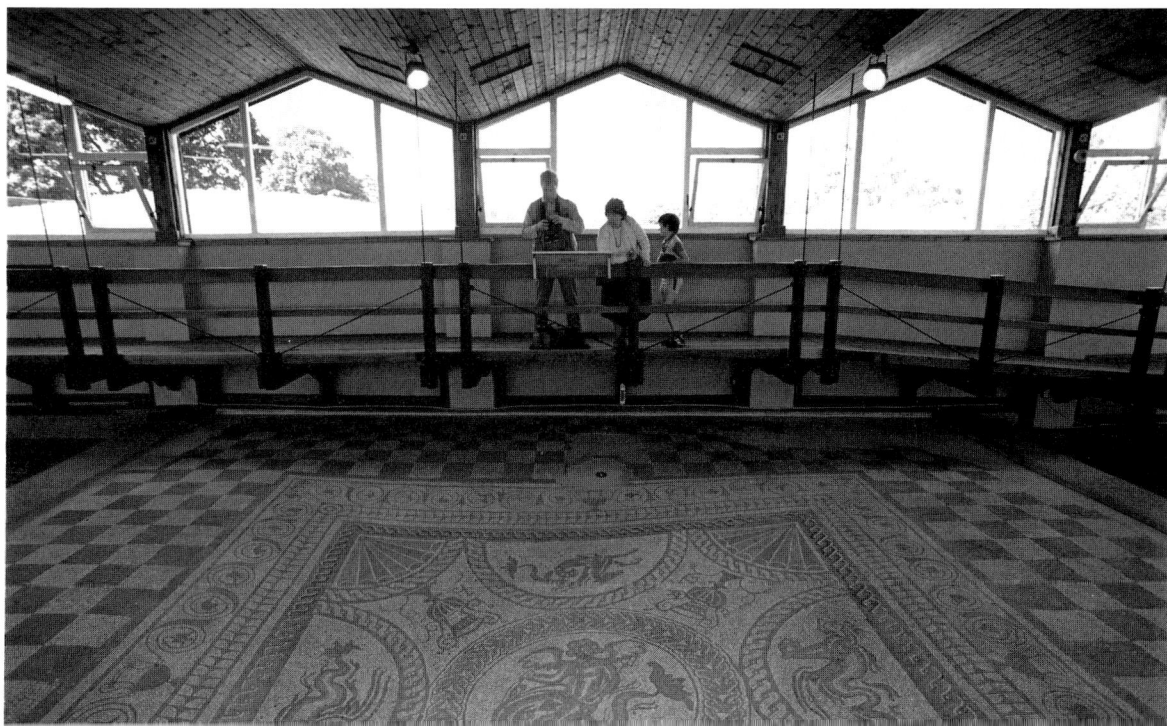

The first-century A.D. villa or, to be more exact, the palace at Fishbourne is a building unparalleled outside Italy at this time, and there is nothing remotely comparable to it in Britain until the fourth century A.D. No traveller in search of Roman Britain should miss the chance to see the remains of the north wing and the elegant reconstructed garden.

What you will see today, however, only represents the final stages in the site's intriguing history. At the time of the Roman invasion, there was a small inlet here with sea access suitable for use as a harbour. Since the native Britons in the surrounding area, under their king, Cogidubnus, were friendly, it is not surprising that the legions used the harbour and erected a group of timber granaries from which campaigning troops were doubtless provisioned. The granaries were succeeded by a timber dwelling of some pretension with painted plaster walls, but in about A.D. 65, this was replaced by the so-called "proto-palace", a substantial courtyarded building with a bath house and lavish architectural details, including a colonnade with columns bearing Corinthian capitals.

FISHBOURNE Sussex
OS 197 SU 839048
The palace is 1¼ miles west of Chichester on the A27 to Portsmouth.

Splendid viewing facilities for the visitor also provide important protection for the priceless mosaics at Fishbourne.

57

Impressive though the "proto-palace" must have been, it was, in turn, dwarfed by the palace proper built some ten years later. This occupied 10 acres and consisted of four large ranges of rooms on each side of a formal garden court. To the south of the southern range, which was probably the main living quarters, there was another formal garden which ran down to the sea. The entrance was in the eastern range where there was a vast entrance hall, and opposite it, in the western range, was the so-called audience chamber. It is this room which suggests that the owner had a political role to play and has led to the inevitable association of Fishbourne with Cogidubnus. We know relatively little of Cogidubnus's career, however. If, as implied by Tacitus, he was installed as a king at the time of the Roman invasion, he would have been relatively elderly by the mid-70s and Tacitus indicates he was dead before A.D. 78. The question of Fishbourne's resident, therefore, remains open.

You can see aspects of Fishbourne's history in the display building covering the northern range. It is suggested that, originally, this was for the accommodation of guests and its basic structure was of suites of small rooms ranged around two small enclosed colonnaded courtyards. In around A.D. 100, there is evidence that the palace was broken up into smaller self-contained dwellings which would explain the addition of a new bath suite at the east end of the northern range to complement that in the southern range. In the mid-second century A.D., the eastern half of the northern range was pulled down and another bath suite erected in the northern part of the east range. Further additions were taking place in the late third century A.D., including the insertion of the fine hypocaust you see immediately on entering the display area when the whole palace was evidently destroyed by fire.

The great attraction of the site today is, of course, the mosaics, but remember they are not all of the same date. The first-century A.D. originals include one which is of considerable interest as it shows a crenellated town wall, with double portalled gates, which encloses a stylized street grid. This must be the first representation of a town ever seen in Britain and clearly indicates the Mediterranean flavour of the palace. Other early mosaics have elegant black on white or, in one case, white on black – designs fashionable in Italy at the time. One of the second-century A.D. mosaics has, as one might expect given the palace's location, an aquatic theme with cupid riding on a dolphin, and this is echoed in a third-century A.D. design showing a central knot surrounded by vases and fish with scallop shells in the corner. The mosaics and the other internal decorative features, including expensive imported marble facings and the most unusual stucco work, were clearly the work of craftsmen brought, no doubt at great expense, from abroad. If Fishbourne were intended to be a showcase of Roman taste, it would have succeeded in the most stylish fashion.

See **Chichester, Villas.**

A sample of the many fine floors in Fishbourne's Roman Palace.

GLOUCESTER (Glevum)
Gloucestershire
OS 162 SO 830180
The city is 104 miles west of London. Take the M40 to Oxford and then the A40. Be sure to visit the cathedral, where Edward II is buried, and the attractive close.

The first Roman presence in the Gloucester area, guarding an important crossing of the River Severn, was a fortress at Kingsholm about 1 mile north of the present town centre. It was probably built by the Twentieth Legion and used as a base for the first sorties into south Wales. in the late 60s, the fortress was moved by the Second Legion Augusta to the site which has become the heart of modern Gloucester.

The life of the fortress was brief, as by the mid-70s the legion had taken a more forward position in Wales at Caerleon but, in about 96–8 A.D., a *colonia* for retired legionaries was founded here reusing, as at the *colonia* in Lincoln founded at the same time, the military defences and some of the fortress streets. Travellers visiting Gloucester today should remember that the four main thoroughfares of the city, simply named Northgate, Eastgate, Southgate and Westgate Streets, have a history of almost 2,000 years.

Unfortunately, Gloucester has suffered more perhaps than any other historic town in Britain from the ravages of modern development. Roman remains can, therefore, only be seen in two places: at the east gate outside Boots' store, and where some wall survives in the City Museum in Brunswick Street. The museum also has a good collection of antiquities, including the tombstones of Rufus Sita, a Thracian cavalryman depicted spearing a barbarian in the usual fashion, and (found in Cirencester) Philus from the Sequani tribe, who lived around Besançon in France. He may have come to the Gloucester area as a merchant. Notice also a stone male head which has curly hair in the Roman style of the first century A.D., but large bulging eyes in the native Celtic style.
See **Towns.**

GREAT WITCOMBE
Gloucestershire
OS 163 SO 900143
The villa is about 5 miles east of Gloucester at the end of a track signposted off the A436, a short distance to the west of the turning to Great Witcombe itself. There is a car park just before the site.

The Roman villa at Great Witcombe has survived less well than the source of its spring water, which still bubbles merrily on.

The site of Great Witcombe villa illustrates, as well as any, the Roman taste for locating country houses in agreeable and attractive surroundings. The buildings were terraced into a south-facing slope and occupy three sides of a courtyard. The principal living rooms in the central range would have commanded splendid views of the plain in which Gloucester lies. Visitors today will, on a clear day, see the tower of Gloucester Cathedral where, in Roman times, one would have seen the Roman *colonia*. Apart from the view, the main reason for the villa's location is a ready water supply from a spring which still exists. In a villa, water was required for a variety of domestic and agricultural purposes but, in particular, for the baths. There was a small suite in the south-west wing at Witcombe of which the remains are preserved in two sheds. They include a *frigidarium*, with accompanying mosaic, and a hot plunge bath. Behind the baths, is an unusual room with three niches in one wall which may have contained votive statues.

The villa has a typical winged-corridor plan and was probably constructed in the mid-third century A.D. with alterations being made in the later third century. Much of the building was probably two storeyed and this explains the large buttresses against the south-east wall of the central range and north-east wing. Notice also the small rectangular room, which later became polygonal, on the north-west side of the central range. It may have contained a shrine to the household gods, or *lares*, much revered in Roman families.
See **Chedworth, Villas.**

59

Daily Life
Society, Fashion and Food

It is no easier to say what was typical in the life of a Roman Briton than it is to say what is typical in the life of today's Britons. Not only were there great changes over the 350 years of the Roman era, but the way people lived was very much dependent on their social standing which, in turn, related to wealth and the circumstances of birth.

At the top of the social scale were people associated with the legions, the provincial administration, the government of towns and those who had prospered in commerce. They were, by and large, Roman citizens which gave them a whole series of legal privileges not accorded to the majority of the population. Even after the extension of citizenship to all free-born inhabitants of the empire by the Emperor Caracalla in A.D. 212, social and legal distinctions remained just as rigid between the upper rank of citizens known as *honestiores* and the masses who were known as *humiliores*.

At the bottom of the social scale were the slaves. Slavery was a common institution in ancient societies and the Romans did not introduce it to Britain. In fact, Britain was known as an exporter of slaves to the empire. The lot of the slave varied considerably depending on the status of his or her owner. Some slaves worked in the mines or in industry, others were in domestic service. Others again, however, might occupy important government posts. There is, for example, the tombstone of a woman called Claudia Martina from London which was set up by her husband Anencletus who was a "slave of the province", meaning that he was on the governor's staff and so a man of sufficient status to marry a woman who was herself a citizen.

On the whole, a close bond seems to have existed between master and slave, as is shown in one of Martial's epigrams:

> To you my parents, I send on
> This little girl Erotion,
> The slave I loved, that by your side
> Her ghost need not be terrified.

Most slaves could look forward to getting their freedom at some stage and this created another intermediate social class of freemen and women. Freedmen often continued to work in their former master's business and saw to his affairs after his death, while erecting for him a suitable tombstone. A good example of a freedwoman is Regina whose tombstone can be seen at South Shields. She had evidently married a Palmyran dealer in flags and it is possible that he was once her master.

Another important social distinction was that between the sexes. Roman society was strongly patriarchal, although by the time of the early empire the absolute power of husbands over their wives had lessened and divorce had become much easier. Women were, however, banned from holding any public office and their rights to own property were limited. On the other hand, there is no reason to suppose that women were subservient; many of the empresses were strong characters who wielded great authority in their own right and, at a humbler level, many women must have assisted their husbands in business or other work. Skeletal evidence certainly shows that the majority of Romano-British women engaged just as much in heavy physical labour as the men.

One of a Roman woman's principal roles, of course, was as a mother which was extremely hazardous in those days of primitive obstetrics, and death in childbirth probably accounts for the lower expectation of life of women as opposed to men. It is not necessarily the case, however, that women had large numbers of children, since relatively poor nutrition might have meant they were less fertile and arrived at maturity later than is normal today. Claudia Rufina, a British woman whose charm attracted Martial, was also praised by him as, unusually, the bearer of three children.

Children were obviously much loved in Roman times to judge, for example from two touching epitaphs on tombstones from York. One was dedicated to 13-year-old Corellia Optata by her father who says: "Ye hidden spirits that dwell in Pluto's Acherusian realms, whom the scanty ash and the shade, the body's image, seek after life's little day, I, the pitiable father of an innocent daughter, caught by cheating hope lament her final end." The other just reads: "For Simplicia Florentina a most innocent soul who lived ten months, Felicius Simplex her father . . . had this made." In spite of these touching words, however, one cannot help wondering whether a certain fatalism over the fate of children did not prevail when infant mortality approached 40 per cent and there is some evidence that they were not really considered as individuals until their first teeth showed.

One of the most important indicators of class and other social differences was probably dress. Unfortunately, however, we only have good information for what the upper classes wore, since they were the people who could afford sculptured funerary monuments.

Although Tacitus says that, "The toga was everywhere to be seen" in the governorship of Agricola, there is little evidence that this traditional mark of the Roman citizen was widely worn in Britain. The problem was that the toga was quite a difficult garment to put on, requiring the services of a slave to get all the folds in the right place. Even in Rome it seems its popularity was waning by the second century A.D. The basic garment in Britain was evidently a tunic, made either of linen or wool, which came down to around the knees and was held by a belt at the waist. Workmen, such as the smith shown on the tombstone from York, wore a short version of it, but although there is some evidence for woollen stockings no one wore trousers which were considered only fit for barbarians. Women also wore tunics under a more voluminous garment, or *stola*, which is what, for example, Regina at South Shields is wearing. Over their tunics and *stolae*, people wore a variety of cloaks, such as one which was usually about knee length or longer and fastened at the throat. For bad weather thick woollen hooded cloaks were worn, such as that shown on Philo's tombstone in Gloucester Museum.

Shoes often survive in archaeological deposits, and one of the commonest types is the *calceus* which has leather soles and uppers with laces which tied at the ankles. Soldiers would wear a *caliga*, a sandal kept in place with straps across the foot and thongs wound around the ankle and up the calves. The soles of these shoes consist of layers of leather held together by dome-headed nails which, incidentally, suggests that buildings or streets full of people were constantly echoing to the sound of clicking and scraping. Lighter openwork sandals with the leather cut and stamped in patterns are also known to have been worn by men and women, and among the shoes found at Vindolanda is a wooden-soled shoe which may have been used to walk on the hot floor of the baths.

One of the most diverse and rapidly changing aspects of fashion in Roman times appears to have been the treatment of hair. Styles were set by the imperial court and can be traced on the coinage. In the first century A.D., therefore, men appear to have very simple haircuts, although Nero went in for extravagant coiffures, but in the second century A.D. artificially curled hair, which might be dyed and perfumed, became popular. A man usually had his hair cut in a barber's shop where he could also be shaved, but the quality of razors was not what we are used to and so there was no doubt relief when the fashion demanded beards, as it did, for example, when Hadrian succeeded Trajan.

Women in the first century A.D. also had simple hair-styles, until the latter part when some very elaborate structures appeared with masses of probably false curls mounted on a wire structure at the front of the head. This can be clearly seen on coins of Julia, daughter of the Emperor Titus. In the mid-second century A.D. styles were rather less elaborate: hair was heavily waved and plaited and gathered at the back or wrapped around the head, Variations on the arrangement of the plaits and chignons continue to appear on the heads of the early-third-century A.D. empresses which are to some extent reflected on representations of British women. Hair in whatever fashion, however, would have been held in place with hair pins and they occur in numbers on archaeological sites and can be seen in many museums.

Another aspect of daily life in which behaviour probably varied according to social class was the taking of meals, although we are very much dependent for information on literary sources which describe the habits of the upper classes in Rome itself. It appears, however, that breakfast and the midday meal were relatively light, while the main meal of the day was the *cena* in the evening, after the day's work or entertainments.

In polite society it was served in the *triclinium*, or dining room, the name being derived from the padded couches which had three places for diners to recline while they ate. Eating while sitting was only for children and slaves. The couches were ranged around a low table where knives and spoons might be provided with the food, although people usually used their hands. Among the lower orders there was probably less decorum, but their manners must have changed somewhat as new types of pottery vessel – such as bowls, flagons, and small cups and plates – became commonplace in the Roman period.

As we know from works like *The Satyricon* by Petronius, Roman banquets could be monuments to gluttony and excess, but simpler meals are also known, such as that served by Juvenal to a friend which included:

big straw packed eggs
Still warm from the nest, and the pullets that laid them, and grapes
Preserved for six months, but as fresh as when they were gathered;
Baskets of Syrian pears and Italian Bergamots, fragrant
Apples, the equal of any you'd find in an east coast orchard . . .

For Britain, literary evidence is virtually confined to the Vindolanda writing tablets which record supplies of meats, wines and beer to the garrison, but archaeology has now produced a substantial amount of evidence for diet largely in the form of bones thrown in rubbish pits or open middens. Meat was clearly in good supply, with beef predominant, but mutton and pork, including sucking pig, were also popular. The evidence for wild animals is relatively scarce. The fish eaten were rather different from today, in the sense that there was no deep-sea fishing and the rivers were cleaner. Salmon was common, therefore, and so were herring which were caught offshore in places such as the Thames estuary. Fish sauce, *garum*, was considered a great delicacy and came to Britain in large jars, or *amphorae*, and as anyone who has dug on a Roman site will know, oysters must have been consumed in large quantities. Sadly, they have now been driven out by pollution.

Bread was, of course, the major source of carbohydrate and we may imagine that it was what we would call the granary or wholemeal variety, often with a lot of grit in it as the corn was ground with stone querns. Grit would have worn the Romano-British teeth down, but dental caries seems to have been rare as they were spared the damaging high-sugar foods we eat today.
See **York.**

HADRIAN'S WALL

*The Roman frontier runs across
northern England through the
counties of Northumberland and
Cumbria from Wallsend, on the
Tyne, to Bowness-on-Solway.
Travellers wishing to visit the sites
along it are recommended to make
first for Newcastle in the east or
Carlisle in the west according to the
directions given in the site entries.*

No traveller studying the remains of Roman Britain can fail to be impressed by Hadrian's Wall. Not only is it a monument unique in the Roman world, but it is, for the most part, to be found in some of Britain's most dramatic and beautiful countryside. The history of the Wall is, however, complex and not always easy to understand from the visible structures.

In the first forty years or so of Roman rule, the imperial government had probably every intention of conquering the whole of Britain, indeed, it was regarded by men like Agricola, governor of Britain from A.D. 78–84, as something of a sacred duty for the empire to absorb the known world and endow it with Roman culture. Agricola, therefore, campaigned vigorously in Scotland and was doubtless planning for complete conquest when he was retired. Shortly afterwards, one of the legions in Britain was withdrawn and it became necessary to set a northern limit to the province. A frontier between the Tyne and the Solway was, therefore, established early in the reign of Trajan (A.D. 98–117), along the line of a road known as the Stanegate between forts at Corbridge in the east and Carlisle in the west. Between them there were five other forts, of which the best-known is at Chesterholm (Vindolanda).

In A.D. 117, Hadrian succeeded Trajan and his visit to Britain in A.D. 122 was part of an empire-wide tour to create peaceful and stable borders. In effect, he abandoned the aim

Above left, Emperor Hadrian wisely chose to reinforce the natural obstacles in this spectacular landscape to the east of Housesteads with his formidable wall. Above, Sewingshields Milecastle.

of world conquest and, in Britain, designed a permanent frontier to "divide Rome from the barbarians", as his biographer puts it. As initially designed, the frontier was a wall set forward from the Stanegate, which ran from Newcastle upon Tyne in the east to Bowness-on-Solway in the west – about 66 miles. East of the River Irthing, it was built of stone; west of the Irthing, it was built of turf. In front of the Wall there was a V-profile ditch except in the central Winshields sector where the cliff face was sufficient defence. At 1 mile intervals, there were fortlets known as milecastles built in stone on the stone wall and in turf and timber on the turf wall. Between each milecastle were two turrets, essentially fortified gateways built in stone throughout. Construction work was by the legions, possibly with the help of local forced labour.

Before this design was fully executed, however, it became clear that it was unsatisfactory and that the main body of troops needed readier access to the area north of the Wall. A series of forts were, therefore, constructed on the Wall line between about A.D. 126 and A.D. 138. The largest fort – and presumably the seat of the commander of the Wall garrison, some 10,000 men at its height – was at Stanwix near Carlisle. Another alteration of this period was the addition of the Vallum, a flat-bottomed ditch with a mound on either side, which runs behind the Wall giving it extra security from the rear. Opposite the forts, causeways were left which were guarded by a gateway, the best surviving example being at Benwell. Thirdly, there was a reduction in the width of the Wall from the originally planned 10 feet (known as the Broad Wall) to 8 feet or less (known as the Narrow Wall).

Although the Roman army preferred to tackle an enemy by fighting in the field, we need only to see the reconstructed section of the Wall at Vindolanda to realize that the Wall's purpose was essentially military – to defend the Roman province from the unwelcome intrusions of barbarians. As the antiquary, William Hutton, put it in 1801: "That a man is born a savage, there needs no other proof than Severus's Wall (as it was known then). It characterises two nations as robbers and murderers." Part of the scheme must also have been the creation of a buffer zone made up of a Romanized population and, judging by the growth of towns at Carlisle and Corbridge and of the *vici* outside other forts, this was a success.

No sooner was the Wall completed, than Hadrian was succeeded by Antonius Pius and it was abandoned in favour of a new frontier between the Forth and the Clyde: the Antonine Wall. It was not until the mid-160s that Hadrian's Wall was permanently regarrisoned and it then remained the permanent northern limit of the empire until the end of the Romano-British era. In the later second century A.D., modifications to the design continued: the reconstruction of the turf wall in stone was completed and a road known as the Military Way was built between the Vallum and the Wall linking the stations along it. Many of the turrets, such as Coesike and Piper Sike, were abandoned.

Further reconstruction on the Wall took place during the the reign of the Emperor Septimius Severus (A.D. 193–212) occasioned, perhaps, both by damage recorded in the mid-180s by barbarian raids and by neglect, if not destruction, following the withdrawal of troops from Britain by the governor Clodius Albinus, to assist his challenge for the throne. This work included repairs to forts, such as Birdoswald, and to the Wall itself. Recent excavations at Castle Nick, near Housesteads, suggest that in places it may have been rebuilt from the foundations up and so here it is more accurately Severus's Wall, as Hutton called it. Severus also embarked on major construction work at Corbridge and South Shields preparatory to his campaigns in Scotland.

The third century A.D. was largely a period of peace on the Wall; the Vallum fell out of use and civilian *vici* grew up outside the fort walls. Severus had, at last, formally allowed soldiers to marry and their wives and families probably formed a major component of the settlements.

By A.D. 296, when Constantius Chlorus visited Britain after defeating the usurper Allectus, it seems that many forts were, in part, abandoned and their buildings had fallen into disrepair – "covered with earth and fallen into ruin", as an inscription from Birdoswald puts it. Constantius, therefore, initiated rebuilding work at a number of sites. A feature of the forts in the fourth century A.D. appears to be barracks reconstructed into roomier self-contained "chalets". This probably reflects the fact that the frontier forces, *limitanei*, were now officially permanent on the Wall rather than potentially movable as they were then the empire was still expanding.

The fate of the Wall in the last years of Roman Britain is difficult to trace because of the sparseness of features which can be dated, but the last period of major reconstruction probably followed the Barbarian Conspiracy of A.D. 367 when Count Theodosius was sent to Britain. Subsequent to this, the garrison probably gradually disappeared, as successive would-be emperors drained the country of troops, until there were few soldiers worthy of the name on the Wall by the early fifth century A.D.

See **The Army, Emperors in Britain.**

HADRIAN'S WALL
South Shields (Arbeia)
Tyne and Wear
OS 88 NZ 366678
South Shields is on the south bank of the Tyne, some 11 miles east of Newcastle. The park in which the Roman remains are to be found lies on the north side of the town centre. When approaching on the A185 from Newcastle, or the A194 from the A1, it is best to take the road which runs along the bank of the Tyne until you see a sign to the Roman Fort.

A good supply system was one foundation of the Roman army's phenomenal success and it is in this context that we should understand the role of South Shields fort, the easternmost installation in the Hadrian's Wall frontier system. The fort guarded the mouth of the River Tyne and bulky stores and equipment could have been ferried up the east coast, perhaps from the legionary base at York and then distributed from here under military supervision along the Wall line.

Trade by private merchants also passed through South Shields, as is demonstrated by the tombstone of Regina, now in the site museum, who we know was the wife of Barathes, a man from Palmyra whose tombstone was found at Corbridge. He was apparently a dealer in flags, for which there was doubtless steady demand along the Wall.

Regina is also interesting as she came from the Catuvellauni tribe in south-east England and her tombstone tells us that she was a *liberta*, or freed slave. From very humble origins, therefore, possibly sold into slavery as a girl, she eventually found prosperity with a merchant from the east. One wonders how they met.

Besides supervision of supply transport, more conventional military duties would have been expected of the garrison – in the second century A.D. a cavalry regiment known as the First Ala of Asturians – for Hadrian's Wall was not extended east of Wallsend, leaving the river as the frontier. Another fine tombstone commemorates Victor, who was also a freed slave who had originally belonged to Numerianus, as a member of the regiment.

Remains of the Hadrianic defences can be seen around most of the fort except on the south side, for reasons which will shortly be apparent, and travellers to South Shields will soon see a full-scale reconstruction of the west gate. Little has survived of the original structure but, based on fort gates on Hadrian's Wall and elsewhere, it has been possible to make a reasonable conjecture as to its appearance. This is a most imaginative project which will bring Roman military architecture to life in a way that is all too rare.

In the late second century A.D., the fort was extended southwards, perhaps to accommodate the Fifth Cohort of Gauls known to be here in the third century A.D.. Then, during Septimius Severus's campaigns in Scotland, South Shields came into its own as a supply base. A number of new granaries were built to store provisions for the army and you can see their footings *in situ* today. The original

Hadrianic granary also survives and it evidently had a colonnade facing the *via principalis* and a loading platform at the back. Look also at the *principia*, remodelled in the Severan period, and notice the large sunken storing room at the back where army pay and other valuables were kept.

Severus's campaigns were cut short by his death, and so the new granaries were shortlived and converted into barracks. In the fourth century A.D., the *Notitia Dignitatum* records the garrison as the Numerus Barcariorum Tigrisiensium who were a unit of Tigris boatmen from the other end of the empire in Syria. Their role was to protect the river mouth at a time of increasing seaborne raids on the east coast. The climate can hardly have suited them.
See **Hadrian's Wall, Hadrian's Wall – Corbridge, The Army.**

As originally designed, Hadrian's Wall began at Newcastle; the extension to Wallsend is later. Little is known of any Roman emplacements here, however, although the piers of the Roman bridge (the "Pons"), evidently survived into the 1860s. The other element in the Roman name, "Aelius", is taken from Hadrian's family name and so we have here an unusual example of a place name in Britain which does not incorporate the Latinized version of a native name.

The principal reason for travellers on the trail of the Romans to visit Newcastle today is the Musuem of Antiquities, which has an unparalleled collection of inscribed and sculpted stones from the Wall. All visitors will have their own favourites, but be sure to visit the reconstruction of the Carrawburgh Mithraeum where the original stones are to be

found. You will see how the light would have shone from behind the relief of Mithras, charioteer of the sun, through spaces cut in it to represent rays.

Look out also for the dedication stone from the granary at Benwell, the next fort to the west, which records construction by a detachment of the fleet in the earliest phase of Wall building between A.D. 122 and 124 under the governorship of Platorius Nepos. A more unusual inscription is a metrical hymn constituting a dedication to the Virgin of the Zodiac, who is equated with Julia Domna, Septimius Severus's wife and an enthusiast for oriental religions. The stone comes from Carvoran fort where a detachment of Syrian archers was stationed.
See **Hadrian's Wall, Hadrian's Wall – Carrawburgh, Temples and Religion.**

HADRIAN'S WALL
Newcastle upon Tyne
(Pons Aelius)
Tyne and Wear
OS 88 NZ 250640
The city is 280 miles north of London. If you are travelling by car use the A1, although it is quicker by train from King's Cross Station, London. The Museum of Antiquities is in the university on the north side of the city centre.

Although virtually nothing survives of Benwell fort, it is still possible to appreciate its site on a level plateau overlooking the Tyne Valley, or one might even say Tyne gorge, to the south. We know from an inscription now in the Museum of Antiquities at Newcastle, that construction work was undertaken by men of the British fleet, or Classis Britannica, who must have found suitable anchorage in the river below.

The only military feature to be seen at Benwell is the so-called Vallum Crossing. The Vallum, or great ditch, which served to define the military zone behind Hadrian's Wall, was dug after the Wall forts had been built and so it deviates to avoid them; it was also left undug outside their south gates to allow access. At Benwell, you can see the well-preserved causeway which would have had a monumental arch over it and double gates – the pivot hole for a gate hinge still survives in a stone block. To the north of the causeway, several successive road surfaces have been left exposed.

On the south-east side of the fort there was a small temple whose footings survive in the rather unlikely location of a suburban garden. While on duty, soldiers were expected to take part in official religious ceremonies in which worship of the imperial house and the Capitoline Triad played an important part, but otherwise they were free to worship as they pleased. In the Benwell Temple, the god was known as Antenociticus, or Anociticus, who may either have been a local Celtic deity, or an import by the Benwell garrison which was the First Cohort of Vangiones. The stone head of a cult statue found here is in the Museum of Antiquities, Newcastle, along with the originals of two altars found either side of the apse. One of them was dedicated by Tineius Longus recording his promotion to senatorial rank and *quaestor* designate during the governorship of Ulpius Marcellus in about 180 A.D. Obviously, he was a man on his way to the highest office.
See **Hadrian's Wall, Temples and Religion.**

HADRIAN'S WALL
Benwell
(Condercum)
Tyne and Wear
OS 88 NZ 214647
Benwell today is a suburb of Newcastle, 2 miles west of the city centre on the A69. There are signs on the main road to direct you to both the Vallum Crossing and Temple. The first substantial stretch of Hadrian's Wall, with an accompanying turret, can be seen 1 mile further west at Denton Hall.

HADRIAN'S WALL

Corbridge
(Corstopitum)
Northumberland
OS 87 NY 982648

*Corbridge is 17 miles west of
Newcastle, just off the A69. The
Roman site lies on the west side of
the town and is signposted.*

One of the most important effects of Roman military occupation on the Tyne–Solway frontier was the stimulus it gave to the local economy. Villages grew up outside most of the forts and, on occasions, as at Corbridge, they became flourishing market towns.

Although Corbridge's heyday as a town was in the later Roman period, the site has a history which began between A.D. 87 and A.D. 90 when a fort was built here as part of the Stanegate frontier system which predates Hadrian's Wall. Nothing can now be seen of this fort or of two subsequent forts, as they were built of timber, but in about A.D. 139–40, a stone fort was constructed here and parts of its commanding officer's house can still be seen.

To get an impression of subsequent developments, the traveller should stand on the Stanegate itself which runs east-west through the display area. By the early third century A.D., the regular fort layout seems to have been abandoned and the change-over, first of all to a military supply base, connected like that at South Shields, with the Emperor Septimius Severus's campaigns in the north and then to a town was under way. New buildings included two granaries which had a colonnade fronting onto the north side of the Stanegate. They are among the best preserved in Roman Britain and their raised floors and external buttresses are especially

notable. Next to the granaries is an impressive fountain – testimony to the Roman concern, if not obsession, with adequate water supplies. On the north side of the street also, there is a large building known as the Store House, so-called because it has lots of small rooms ranged around its central courtyard. It was, however, unfinished and its real function remains uncertain.

South of the Stanegate are two enclosed compounds. The western compound contained workshops and the eastern compound officer's houses. Notice how the eastern compound wall carefully avoids the temple buildings on the street frontage. One reason for Corbridge's growth as a town may have been its role as a religious centre and there are a number of fine pieces of religious sculpture in the splendid new site museum. Look out for official dedications to Jupiter, Juno and Minerva (the Capitoline Triad), and to Imperial Discipline and the Regimental Standards. There are also more exotic dedications of an unofficial nature, such as that to Jupiter Dolichenus and the Sky Gods of Brigantia, who were presumably worshipped in the area in pre-Roman times. Finally, be sure to admire the famous Corbridge Lion, a stone sculpture which originally adorned a fountain head.

See **Hadrian's Wall, Temples and Religion.**

Opposite page, top, fragments of masonry outside the site museum which contains many fine figurative carvings and inscriptions from Corstopitum, below, ventilation engineering in a granary. Above left, the smooth cut-outs on a redundant water storage tank are thought to have been created by the repeated honing of a legion of Roman swords. Far left, the army's subterranean strongroom, centre, the remains of the workings of the decorative fountain that was fed with water from the tank shown above, and left, a drainage gulley.

HADRIAN'S WALL
Planetrees
Northumberland
OS 87 NY 935694
The site is on the south side of the B6318 about 1 mile east of its junction with the A6079 from Hexham. It is not easy to find, but look for steps over a stone wall opposite an isolated private house.

The stretch of Hadrian's Wall at Planetrees Farm is of interest because it includes a junction between the Broad Wall, built during the early stages of Wall construction, and a section only 6 feet thick. The foundation is, however, broad throughout suggesting that the reduced thickness was due to a change of plan when rapid completion of the Wall was required in the latter stages of the building campaign.

The preservation of the Wall at this site is due to the entreaties of William Hutton, an antiquary who travelled along the complete line of the Wall in 1801 when aged 78. On arriving at Planetrees, he found a farmer, one Henry Tulip, about to reuse the stones for a farm building. Hutton records that he asked Tulip's workman "to give my compliments to Mr. Tulip and request him to desist, or he would wound the whole body of Antiquaries. As he was putting an end to the most noble monument of Antiquity in the whole Island, they would feel every stroke".
See **Hadrian's Wall.**

Brunton Turret is an excellent example of the great structural strength of these small defensive positions.

A short distance west of Planetrees, you will come to the most westerly stretch of the Broad Wall and a turret east of which is another length of Wall 6 feet wide on the broad foundation. Notice, however, that when the turret was built it was obviously anticipated that the Broad Wall would be constructed throughout at this point as the short turret wing walls are in the broad gauge.

Considerable research has been done on the identity of the legionary detachments who built the different parts of Hadrian's Wall and the emplacements along it. Each of the legions involved – the Second, the Sixth and the Twentieth – had a distinctive building style and the principal features can be worked out on the basis of small inscribed stones which the soldiers left to commemorate their efforts. We know, therefore, that because Brunton Turret has a doorway to the right on its south side and because the Wall here has a single offset course at the base, work in this area was probably undertaken by the Twentieth Legion.

See **Hadrian's Wall.**

HADRIAN'S WALL Brunton
Northumberland
OS 87 NY 923698
The site is indicated by a signpost a little to the south of the junction of the B6318 and A6079.

71

HADRIAN'S WALL

Chesters
(Cilurnum)
Northumberland
OS 87 NY 912702

The fort is to be found on the south side of the B6318 a little to the west of the Chollerford roundabout, which can be reached by taking the A6079 from Hexham and turning left at the crossroads near Brunton turret. The bridge abutment is reached by a path on the east side of the modern bridge carrying the B6318 over the north Tyne.

The fort at Chesters was built across the line of Hadrian's Wall in about A.D. 128 and there is much of interest here for the traveller in pursuit of Roman Britain. The defences, consisting of a rampart, stone wall and double ditch, are easy to trace and all the gates are visible. Notice how the main side gates are set forward of the Wall to allow the troops to ride out to face an attacker at a moment's notice.

Chesters was garrisoned in the third century A.D. by the Second Ala of Asturian cavalry, who had originally come from Spain, and parts of two of their barrack blocks are visible. They would each have held a troop, or *turma*, of sixty-four horsemen; the most spacious quarters at the ends were for the officers. You should also inspect the remains of the *principia*, which has a particularly impressive strong room. This building would originally have been adorned with fine sculpture, including a relief, now in the site museum, on which there is a soldier holding a flag inscribed with a dedication to "the valour of the emperors". The emperors in question are Severus Alexander and the depraved and corrupt Elagabalus, known as Antonius on inscriptions, whose name was erased from the stone after his death. Probably from the *principia* also, and again in the site museum, is a large statue thought to

represent Severus Alexander's mother, Julia Mamaea, as Cybele standing on a heifer. This is another example of the practice of portraying near-eastern empresses of the third century A.D. as goddesses.

To the east of the fort, by the banks of the Tyne, is the bath house which is one of the best preserved in Britain. The usual sequence of rooms is visible but note, in particular, the unusual niches for clothing lockers in the dressing room. There is another small bath house attached to the commandant's house inside the fort, which was probably added in the fourth century A.D. when standards of comfort for the frontier troops were being generally improved.

Finally, be sure to visit the site museum and take time to inspect the huge array of sculpture and inscriptions from Chesters itself and other forts along the Wall. Notice also the unique brass corn measure probably used during collection of the *annona*, or grain tax, paid by native farmers to the military authorities.

Across the Tyne from the fort is the remains of a Roman stone bridge abutment. The bridge itself would have been of timber – an arrangement similar to that at Piercebridge and Willowford.
See **The Army, Public Buildings, Bath Houses.**

Top, the large changing room beyond one of the cold rooms in the bath house close to the banks of the North Tyne. Far left and above, the remains of the bridge abutment on the east bank of the river.

Public Buildings
Business and Pleasure

The public buildings of a Romano-British town were the physical expression of its absorption into the empire's political and social system. Their erection usually took place soon after the laying out of the streets. This strongly suggests official supervision, and it is quite likely that the army was used to oversee construction since the Britons had no tradition of monumental architecture, although the native community leaders were probably expected to pay for the work.

The forum was located in one of the town's central *insulae* in a position analogous to that of a fort *principia*. The form of the two buildings was also similar. A central courtyard was surrounded on three sides by ranges of small rooms often used as shops; in the forum at Wroxeter, for example, the complete stock-in-trade of a pottery seller was found buried by the debris of a fire. On the fourth side of the courtyard stood the basilica, a substantial aisled building usually comparable in size to the nave of a cathedral. In the main cross-hall, public meetings could be held and justice dispensed from the *tribunal*, or "bench", at one end. Beyond the hall would be a series of rooms including the treasury and council chamber, or *curia*. In the central room facing the main entrance there was, as in a fort, the *aedes* containing a shrine to the emperor and perhaps some presiding local deity.

The success of urban development in Roman Britain can, to some extent, be charted by the fate of the forum buildings. In London, for example, the first forum, constructed in about A.D. 80 was relatively small but the second, dating to the reign of Hadrian after some 40 years of rapid growth in the town, was nearly six times as large. Towards the end of the Roman period, however, there is evidence that fora were falling into disrepair or were converted to other uses. By the end of the third century A.D., for example, it appears that metal working was taking place in the basilica at Silchester and in the late fourth century A.D., the forum at Leicester burnt down never to be rebuilt.

The success or failure of a town obviously depended on its economy and so, in an attempt to encourage trade, a special market hall, or *macellum*, might be built. A number have been identified, but the only one presently visible is at Wroxeter where it was originally a two-storied building with small rooms surrounding a courtyard.

Alongside the development of a Romanized political and economic system went the introduction of Romanized social customs. The focus of many of these was the public baths but, since the remains of so many survive, they have been discussed under 'Bath Houses'. Equally important as places of entertainment and relaxation were the amphitheatres. Usually located on the fringes of the settled area, they were essentially rustic versions of the Colosseum and other great Mediterranean amphitheatres. In plan, they were ovoid with an arena surrounded by *cavea*, or banks of seating, retained, perhaps initially, with timber walls later replaced by masonry. At each end of the arena, there was an entrance for the "performers" and on each side a small room for them to change or wait their cue. Above these rooms was the podium or seating for honoured guests. Another component of the arena might be a Nemeseum or shrine to Nemesis, Goddess of Fate or Vengeance, most appropriate for the gladiators. Other breaks in the surrounding seating would be for steps known as *vomitoria*, so-called because of the way they disgorged the spectators at the end of a performance.

Amphitheatres accommodated a variety of activities. In those attached to military centres such as Caerleon they were probably used for drill and manoeuvres, and the observance of official religious ceremonies. In towns they were places for public execution, and the entertainments could be equally gruesome. Animals were slaughtered in bear baiting and mock hunts and there is also evidence for gladiatorial contests in Britain. The so-called Colchester vase shows a combat between a fully armoured gladiator and a man with a net known as a *retiarius*. One of the mosaics from Bignor shows two cupids dressed as gladiators. This pretty scene should not, however, allow us to overlook the unpleasant-ness of the "sport". The combatants were usually prisoners or men con-demned to death, but they might also be procured from the lower ranks of society by a *lanista*, or someone who acted as trainer. The only escape from the ring was usually by murdering one's opponent. The fate of a man defeated but not yet dead depended on the whim of the presiding official, usually under the influence of the spectators. Gambling on the outcome of the contests added a further unsavoury element.

Theatres, as opposed to amphitheatres, were much less common in Britain and the only substantial visible remains are at St Albans. In plan they were usually semi-circular with the *proscaenium*, or stage, on the straight side facing the seating rising in tiers on the curved side. The space between the stage and the seating was known as the *orchestra* where, in classical drama, the chorus danced and sang. It is difficult to tell what sort of shows took place in the theatre, although the proximity of temples again suggests that they were used for religious purposes. Otherwise, the evidence from Rome itself is for light entertainment rather than serious drama and several masks of, perhaps, actors belonging to travelling theatre companies have been found in Britain.

As a final thought, we might remember that following Mediterranean practice, both the amphitheatre and theatre were open air. It is no wonder that the *birrus britannicus* worn by "winter" in the Chedworth *triclinium* mosaic was a hooded cloak.

See **Hadrian's Wall-Chesters, Lincoln, St Albans, Silchester, Towns.**

HADRIAN'S WALL

Carrawburgh
(Brocolita)
Northumberland
OS 87 NY 859711

The site is on the south side of the B6318 about 4 miles west of the Chollerford roundabout and is clearly signposted. Midway between Chesters and Carrawburgh, travellers may care to see a fine piece of Hadrian's Wall and a turret at Black Carts Farm.

Shaded altars to sun god Mithras within the temple at Brocolita.

The fort at Carrawburgh appears today as a grassy platform with a rampart and ditch surrounding it. The defences are especially impressive on the west side, but it is of particular interest that the fort was built over the infilled Vallum which can still be seen to either side of it. The fort is, therefore, later than the Vallum dug in about A.D. 128 and so it is late in the series of forts which were placed on the line of Hadrian's Wall.

The main reason for visiting Carrawburgh today is the Temple of Mithras. As you stand in front of the altars to this savage sun god, you should be aware of the contrast between his Persian homeland and the rugged Northumbrian hills, but the presence of the temple and others like it near many British forts is, of course, explained by Mithraism's appeal to soldiers. The cult devotees progressed through a series of severe initiation rites each time acquiring a new grade, rather like an army rank. The temple, as it stands, consists of an entrance porch and main chamber which has the remains of benches on either side and copies of altars at the north end. The original altars are in a reconstruction of the temple in the Museum of Antiquities in Newcastle. When Christianity became the official religion of the empire in the early fourth century A.D., the Carrawburgh, Mithraeum was evidently destroyed and the "Lord of Light" shone no longer.

In a marshy area a little to the north-west of the Mithraeum lies the site of a well sacred to the Celtic nymph Coventina. It was originally enclosed by a stone-built shrine. Excavations in the well produced large quantities of coins and other offerings. Sculptured reliefs showing the nymph, either singly or in triplicate, can now be seen in Chesters Museum.

See **Hadrian's Wall, Temples and Religion.**

When Hadrian's Wall was planned, the desire for symmetry and regularity often meant fortifications, especially turrets, were placed where they were not strictly needed. Coesike Turret is typical of those abandoned in the late second century A.D. as surplus to requirements. Like Brunton it has wing walls in broad gauge, but when the Wall itself was built here it was in narrow gauge. On abandonment, the recess into the Wall created as part of the turret's interior space, was filled in and the Wall rebuilt. This infilling is still visible as it has sagged slightly. Notice, finally, that both the ditch in front of the Wall and the Vallum behind it are prominent in this area.

See **Hadrian's Wall, Hadrian's Wall – Brunton.**

HADRIAN'S WALL
Coesike
Northumberland
OS 87 NY 821705
The turret is a little over 6 miles west of the Chollerford roundabout and a little over 2 miles west of Carrawburgh. Find the point at which the Vallum and Wall ditch diverge from the B6318. There is a field gate on the north side of the road here, from which it is a short distance to the turret.

Perched on the crest of a ridge above a precipitous drop to the north and a steep slope to the south, Housesteads Fort has one of the most dramatic settings of any Roman site in Britain. Its location was originally determined by the need to guard the Knag Burn defile to the east, but its relative inaccessibility has doubtless led to the good survival of the stone buildings. The traveller will get as good an impression of the layout of a Roman fort here as anywhere in Britain.

Housesteads was built in about A.D. 128 and the remains of an earlier turret, dating to the time when no forts were planned for the Wall, can still be seen. Unlike Chesters, Housesteads does not straddle the Wall line; its north wall and Hadrian's Wall being one and the same. Notice also that the fort's long axis is, unusually, east-west rather than north-south – an arrangement determined by the restricted nature of the site.

Most of the internal buildings to be seen today are in their third- or fourth-century A.D. form. The best place to start your visit is by entering the south gate and walking up the *via principalis*. The first building on the left is the commandant's house and this is followed by the *principia*, which consists of the customary enclosed courtyard, and basilica, with its cross-hall and five rooms at the back. At no other site, perhaps, is the nature of Roman imperialism summed up so neatly, for here is a building of purely Mediterranean inspiration, designed for keeping the inmates cool in a hot climate, transferred almost without concession to one of the coldest and wettest parts of the empire.

Beyond the *principia* are the granaries with the piers which supported the floors still surviving. Of particular interest also is the long building immediately to the east. Excavations has shown that it began life as a normal barrack block, but in the fourth century A.D. it was rebuilt as a row of self-contained

HADRIAN'S WALL
Housesteads
Northumberland
OS 86/87 NY 790688
The fort may be approached along the B6318 from the east or west, or by taking the A69 from Hexham to Bardon Mill (a distance of 12 miles). Turn right here and follow a series of minor roads northwards which bring you to the B6318 a little to the west of Housesteads.

The approach to Housesteads from the west.

Above, remains of the north granary at Housesteads. Right, much of the fort's 20 seat latrine survives.

"chalets", providing more suitable accommodation for soldiers now permanently based on the Wall, rather than moving from base to base as the empire expanded.

In the south-east corner of the fort, you can inspect that vital feature of military life, the communal latrine. When in use, the soldiers would have sat on seats over the sewers on either side. Water to flush them came from a tank immediately to the north-east and there is also a water trough for washing hands.

You might now leave the fort through the east gate and walk around its south side. On your left, you will see grassy terraces running down the slope where buildings of the civilian settlement, or *vicus*, once stood. The reason for its occupation of such awkward terrain was clearly its close association with the fort, both in an economic and a more personal sense, since a major component of the population was probably soldiers' wives and families.

After inspecting the south and west gates, walk the 450 yards west to one of the best preserved milecastles on the Wall, where part of the arch of the north gate and footings of the barracks still survive. This is probably the work of the Second Legion who built their milecastles to have a greater measurement east-west than north-south; the opposite is characteristic of the Sixth and Twentieth Legions. The gateways here are also thought to indicate the Second Legion. Milecastle gateways either have one or two responds for

the arches. Those which have two responds may have piers which lie more or less flush with the milecastle wall or project slightly from it. The former are probably characteristic of the Second Legion and the latter of the Sixth.

See **Hadrian's Wall, The Army.**

Chesterholm, Vindolanda, has become one of the most famous Roman sites in Britain because of the extensive excavation programme undertaken here in recent years and the unique nature of some of the finds, especially the wooden writing tablets.

The first fort on the site, built of timber, dates from before A.D. 90 and was established as part of the Stanegate frontier system. If you approach the site from the west today, the road follows the exact course of the Stanegate. A rather larger fort dates from about A.D. 95 and lasted until around A.D. 125 when the decision was taken to put forts on the line of Hadrian's Wall.

The writing tablets are associated with the second fort and date from around A.D. 100. They are thin slices of wood which were written on in ink, rather than wax tablets on a solid wooden base previously thought to be a more common medium for writing. The information on them gives us a fascinating insight into the everyday life of a Roman fort. There are records of the activities of the soldiers at work in the *fabrica*, or workshops, and engaged in construction. There are references to military dispositions telling us that the garrison here included the Eighth Cohort of Batavians, originally from Holland, and the First Tungrian Cohort of Infantry. Frontier conditions were evidently calm at this time and one tablet refers contemptuously to the

which has been sent to him.

The first stone fort at Vindolanda dates to the late second century A.D. and probably accommodated troops coming south after the abandonment of Scotland. A *vicus* grew up outside the west gate of this fort, but it probably accommodated military personnel rather than civilians – as is normal in such a settlement. Many of the building remains visible today are of this period, including the bath house and the *mansio*, or guest house, for official travellers which also has a small bath house attached to it. Running up to the fort gate is a good-quality paved street.

There seems to have been a period of abandonment at Vindolanda in the mid-third century A.D., abut in the late third century, a new stone fort was built and a second *vicus* grew up outside the west gate. This settlement was less well ordered than the earlier *vicus*, and had more of a civilian village character.

The best-preserved parts of the fort today are largely late third century A.D., and are probably the result of reconstruction by Constantius Chlorus. Notice how the gate arrangements differ here from those in an early Roman fort. There are only two with single portals, and they are not even opposite each other.

While at Vindolanda be sure to see the reconstructions of Hadrian's Wall. There is a

HADRIAN'S WALL
Chesterholm
(Vindolanda)
Northumberland
OS 86/87 NY 771664
Vindolanda may be reached either by a minor road running north from Bardon Mill on the A69; or by turning left at Once Brewed, a little under 3 miles west of Housesteads, and then first left along the line of the Stanegate.

A variety of underfloor systems at Vindolanda.

"Britunculi", or little Britons. Equally absorbing are the accounts for supplies indicating a varied diet of meat, including venison, pork and ham, as well as wine and beer. Some of the tablets are more personal letters, such as that informing a soldier of some clothing, in the form of socks, sandals and underpants, stretch of stone wall with a turret and a stretch of turf with a milecastle gateway. Once you have these fixed in your mind, appreciation of the nature of the barrier on the Tyne–Solway frontier, even where little survives today, will be all the clearer.

See **Hadrian's Wall, The Army, Emperors in Britain.**

Timber and stone reconstructions – a milecastle gateway and a turret.

The landscape at the west end of this stretch of the Wall.

HADRIAN'S WALL

Castle Nick, Winshields,
Caw Gap
Northumberland
OS 86/87 NY 759678–
NY 713666

This section of Hadrian's Wall has car parks at the west end and near the east end, which can be reached by turnings on the north side of the B6318 at Once Brewed north of Bardon Mill, or where a minor road from Haltwhistle (on the A69) reaches the B6318.

This central stretch of Hadrian's Wall has one of the most dramatic settings of any ancient monument in Britain, running, as much of it does, along high crags and steep precipices. It is here that the life of the soldier on the Wall would have been at its loneliest. Except in the most unusual circumstances, the patrols along the wall-walk would have had only the birds for company.

The first place of interest is Castle Nick Milecastle, which is longer north-south than east-west and is thought to be the work of the Twentieth Legion. Recent work on the Wall curtain itself in this area suggests that it may have been in a poor state of repair by the early third century A.D. and was substantially rebuilt by the Emperor Septimius Severus. West of Peel Gap, a short climb brings you to the highest point on the Wall, Winshields, 1,230 feet above sea level. There are fine views in all directions on a clear day, admittedly rare in this part of the world. There is no ditch in front of this section of the Wall since the crags form obstacle enough. How ever, as you descend, the ditch reappears, and, after another turret and milecastle, you come to a second modern road running across the Wall line.

As you go west from here, the Vallum below you to the south shows up prominently. When it was originally cut to reduce access to the Wall emplacements, thereby giving them extra security at the rear, the upcast from the ditch was formed into two mounds, one on either side. These mounds have long ago been levelled in most places, but are still visible here as far as Cawfields Milecastle. Notice also that the Wall has a number of offsets and insets in its south face which vary its thickness somewhat.

See **Hadrian's Wall, Hadrian's Wall – Housesteads.**

Still water at Caw Gap.

Although the principal task of the men garrisoning Cawfields Milecastle was probably to guard Hole Gap to the west, the choice of site also indicates the somewhat arbitrary nature of some of the planning of Hadrian's Wall. There can have been few visitors passing through the frontier here, since there is a sharp drop immediately beyond the milecastle's north gate.

Cawfields is again the work of the Second Legion, as it is longer east-west than north-south and has gates with two responds and piers flush with the Wall.

The central section of Hadrian's Wall comes to an abrupt end here with an awful example of the ravages of modern development, even in this most historic of landscapes, thanks to a quarry which has created a huge gash in the crags removing a substantial stretch of Wall in the process.

See **Hadrian's Wall, Hadrian's Wall – Housesteads, Hadrian's Wall – Poltross Burn.**

HADRIAN'S WALL
Cawfields Milecastle
Northumberland
OS 86/87 NY 759678
Directions as for the west end of the stretch of Wall referred to above.

Bath Houses
Public Expense and Private Pleasure

Bath houses form one of the commonest types of Roman building to survive in Britain since they were almost invariably built of stone to avoid the danger of fire from the furnaces and the warping of structural timbers by steam. Travellers will, therefore, find military bath houses at places such as Caerleon and Chester; monumental urban public baths at Leicester and Wroxeter, and more intimate facilities in a town house at Dorchester and in villas including Chedworth and Rockbourne.

The baths were introduced to Britain as one of the benefits of the Roman way of life although Tacitus, in his biography of Agricola, refers to them as a "demoralizing temptation". Bathing, however, lay at the heart of Roman social life. It was not just a means of getting clean, but of passing pleasant leisure hours and may even, on occasions, have had something of a religious significance. Those using the baths at Aquae Sulis (Bath) probably attributed the curative properties of the waters to the influence of the presiding deity.

The Roman method of washing themselves did not involve the use of soap but rather the body's natural perspiration mechanisms. On entering the baths they would first strip off in the *apodyterium*, or changing room, and then go into a heated room, or *sudatorium*, to sweat. The next stage was to visit the *caldarium*, also a hot room, where the dirt released by the opening of the skin's pores was removed with a metal tool known as a *strigil*. A prosperous bather would doubtless have had slaves or attendants to help him with this. They might then repair to the *tepidarium*, a warm but not hot room to cool off before taking a plunge in the *frigidarium*, or cold bath, to close the pores again. A pleasant conclusion would be a massage with perfumes and oil. The baths might also offer a *laconicum* which would give dry heat equivalent to a modern sauna. Another facility frequently found in larger bath houses was the *palaestra*, or exercise hall, where bathers could wrestle or indulge in a variety of ball games. Gambling on board games was also popular and in the Roman sewer excavated in York which served the fortress baths, a number of counters were found probably from a game akin to draughts, known as *ludus latrunculorum*.

A generally lively atmosphere clearly prevailed in the baths and this has been evocatively captured by the writer Seneca:

When your strenuous gentleman, for example, is exercising himself by flourishing lead weights; when he is working hard or else pretends to be working hard, I can hear him grunt; and whenever he releases his imprisoned breath, I can hear him panting in wheezy and high pitched tones. Or perhaps I notice some lazy fellow content with a cheap rub-down and hear the crack of a pummelling hand on his shoulder, varying in sound according as the hand is laid on flat or hollow . . . Add to this the arresting of an occasional roisterer or pickpocket, the racket of the man who always likes to hear his own voice in the bathroom, or the enthusiast who plunges into the swimming tank with unconscionable noise and splashing. Then the cake seller with his varied cries, the sausage man, the confectioner and all the vendors of food hawking their wares . . .

Immoral behaviour is also well documented in the baths of the Roman Empire. Procurers and prostitutes haunted them and the opportunities provided by mixed bathing led to many scandals. Women who wished to, could bathe at different times to the men, but many seem to have been keen to join the men in the *palaestra* games. Eventually Hadrian forbade mixed bathing in public establishments, but the inconvenience this caused may account for the extension of some baths in the early second century A.D., including Bath where a number of new rooms were added at this time. The construction of the public baths with their masonry walls (often rendered with plaster mixed with crushed brick for damp-proofing), exterior colonnades, vaulted roofs and elaborate hypocaust, water supply and drainage system was a most sophisticated engineering task and, in the early years, town councils probably had to call on military expertise. Decoration would have required imported craftsmen.

Once the baths had been constructed, the provision of water was probably the biggest ongoing problem with many thousands of gallons required every day for a complex like that, for example, at Wroxeter. Although domestic water would usually be taken from wells or local streams and rivers, larger quantities were brought by aqueduct from a regular spring source. Aqueducts are known from a number of towns and military sites, often running over many miles, either as open channels or occasionally as closed pipes, although there was nothing in Britain comparable to the great stone-built structures of the Mediterranean world, such as the Pont du Gard in southern France. The usual principle governing the working of an aqueduct was gravity: the water came from a source above the town or fort and was then collected in cisterns or a water tower to be distributed as required.

In Rome a recognition of the importance of the baths in people's lives led the emperors to provide them at state expense and allowed free access to all. In provincial towns this duty would have fallen on the town council and clearly involved no small outlay. Indeed this was the sort of burden which seems, in the later Roman period, to have deterred the wealthy from living in towns where they might have had to serve as *decurions*. It is of some interest, therefore, that in the fourth century A.D., at a time when public baths seem to have started going out of use, the construction of bath houses in the villas of the wealthy was enjoying a particular vogue.

See **Bath, Caerleon, Chedworth, Hadrian's Wall – Chesters, Rockbourne, Wroxeter, Towns.**

HADRIAN'S WALL
Greatchesters
(Aesica)
Northumberland
OS 86/87 NY 703668
The fort is 2 miles north of Haltwhistle on the A64 and may be reached either by taking a minor road leading north off the B6318, or by going to the Cawfields car park. From here you should return to and cross the nearby bridge and then follow the direction indicated by the sign saying. "Pennine Way". This involves a ½ mile walk across fields, but there are dramatic views of the Wall behind and of the fort in front of you.

Greatchesters today is one of the less accessible forts on Hadrian's Wall and until recently the Roman remains were in a poor state of repair but, happily, at the time of writing clearance of undergrowth prior to consolidation was in progress.

The location of the fort is, like that of Caw-

fields Milecastle, determined by the need to guard the Caw Gap to the east and this also explains why the fort faces east rather than north, which is normal on the Wall. The defences can be easily traced except in the north-east corner where there is a modern farmhouse. The walls survive best on the

south and west side, where there are no less than four ditches – the ground being level here and providing no natural protection.

The west gate is of particular interest because the blocking, by which it was reduced to a single portal and then closed altogether, is still visible. At other forts, the blocking has usually been removed by the excavators. The dating of these gate blockings is difficult to determine but they should probably relate to the changing posture of the army. In the second century A.D. it did not normally expect to defend the forts and plenty of gates were needed to allow the troops out quickly to fight in the field. In the later Roman period, forts came to be seen much more as strong points to which the army could retreat and, if necessary, withstand a siege so the fewer breachable openings in the walls, the better.

The only internal structures visible at Greatchesters are the footings of some barracks and the vault for the *principia* strongroom. Travellers may find it of interest, however, to use their O.S. maps to trace an aqueduct which runs for some distance over a tortuous course to the north and east of the fort.

See **Hadrian's Wall, The Army.**

Far left, they still gamble in the south gatehouse at Greatchesters. Above, remains of the west gate, and left, the north side of the fort, on line with the Pennine Way.

HADRIAN'S WALL

Walltown Crag
Northumberland
OS 86/87 NY 674664

To reach this stretch of Hadrian's Wall, take the B6318 east from its junction with the A69 at Greenhead (19 miles east of Carlisle). Turn left after about ½ a mile and follow the signs.

Walltown Turret.

The stretch of Hadrian's Wall to be found in Walltown Crag is one of the finest to be seen anywhere, and of particular interest is Walltown Turret. Remarkably, this was built free-standing before the Wall itself was constructed and the butt-joint between Wall and turret can be clearly seen. It has been suggested that it originally served as an observation tower in the early days of the Wall to protect troops engaged in surveying and other preliminary work. To the west of the turret, as at Cawfields, there is another unfortunate quarrying incursion on the Wall line.

While visiting this sector of the Wall, you will find it of interest to visit the Roman Army Museum at Carvoran, which includes a good audio-visual presentation by Robin Birley, excavator of Chesterholm (Vindolanda). The fort at Carvoran lies behind the museum, but there is only a low grassy mound to be seen. Its location is, however, of interest not only as it, unusually, lies to the south of the Vallum, but also because it is at the junction of the Stanegate and the so-called Maiden Way, a road which runs south to Whitly Castle. After Carvoran, the character of the countryside to the west changes, as William Hutton put it: "I have now done with desolate mountains, precipices and climbing stone walls."

HADRIAN'S WALL

Poltross Burn
Cumbria
OS 86 NY 634662

The milecastle lies in the village of Gilsland which is on the B6318 about 2 miles west of its junction with the A69 at Greenhead. On entering the village from the east, turn left immediately before the railway bridge and follow the signs to the site.

Some debate will always surround the original height of Hadrian's Wall, but in the north-east corner of Poltross Burn Milecastle, there are the remains of a staircase which originally led to the rampart walkway and enough survives to allow a projection of 14 or 15 feet to that level. We might then estimate a further 5 or 6 feet to the top of the parapet, making about 20 feet in all.

From the walkway, the troops would have had a splendid view of the Burn to the east, and to the west lay the valley of the Irthing, but it is difficult to assess the lie of the land in this direction today because of a modern railway embankment.

In addition to the stairs, the milecastle has a number of other important features which make it one of the most interesting on the Wall. Its wing walls were built to the broad gauge which demonstrates that it was built before the Wall curtain which is narrow gauge, albeit on broad foundations. The construction of the milecastle and Wall here are the work of the Sixth Legion. The milecastle is longer north-south than east-west; the gates have two responds; and the piers on the interior project from the enclosure wall. Notice the late second-century A.D. wall narrowing the north gate. The Wall has three offset courses at the base, as opposed to one where the other legions worked.

Within the milecastle there are the remains of barracks. Originally each had four rooms and, on the basis of eight men to a room, the garrison would have numbered sixty-four. *See* **Hadrian's Wall, Hadrian's Wall – Housesteads, Hadrian's Wall – Cawfields.**

Above, the base of the staircase which gives the unique clue to the original height of Hadrian's Wall. Left, the milecastle here housed some sixty-four men.

HADRIAN'S WALL

Willowford Cumbria
OS 86 NY 625665

The site is reached by taking the minor road to Low Row in Gilsland village for a short way. Park your car opposite the Ancient Monument sign and walk to the site.

Surprisingly, little is known about bridges in Roman Britain; the principal reason being that their superstructure would usually have been entirely of timber and so, of course, has not survived. Bridge supports – either simple piles driven into the river bed or more substantial piers of masonry or timber – may survive, but unless the course of a river has shifted they will be buried deep in mud and silt. There are only three places, therefore, where extensive remains of Roman bridges can be seen in this country: Willowford, Chesters and Piercebridge. At Willowford the River Irthing was clearly shifting north-west in Roman times and has shifted since, leaving stone work surviving on the east bank.

After leaving the Upper Denton Road and passing a good stretch of the narrow gauge Wall on broad foundations, you eventually pass through a farmyard and descend into the river plain. The first bridge-related feature you come to is the base of a tower, go past it and you will see the site of a smaller tower which once marked the end of the Wall at the river bank and guarded the abutment of the original bridge, now represented by a V-shaped foundation. Subsequently, the tower was demolished and the Wall was extended west, perhaps following a shift in the river, to terminate over a pair of culverts possibly connected with a mill-race. The V-shaped abutment was then widened and another bridge pier west of it was built; between them there is another culvert. At some stage, the larger tower, whose footings you come across first, was added.

As initially constructed, Hadrian's Wall was built in stone only as far west as the Irthing; from here onwards it was built of turf.
See **Hadrian's Wall, Hadrian's Wall–Chesters, Piercebridge.**

Far left and above, the massive scale of the bridge abutment at Willowford. Left, narrow gauge wall built on broad foundations.

HADRIAN'S WALL
Birdoswald
(Camboglanna) Cumbria
OS 86 NY 616663

The fort may be reached either from the east by taking the B6318 west from Gilsland, and then turning left after a mile or so; or from the west by going 2 miles east along the minor road from Banks East turrets.

Barbarians have had rather a bad time at the hands of archaeologists in recent years. Many episodes in Romano-British history once thought to represent the destruction of military installations, as a result of incursions by hostile tribesmen, have been reinterpreted as periods of neglect by the Roman army itself. Barbarian raiders were certainly interested in loot, so the argument goes, but not in taking the time to bring in heavy lifting gear to demolish stone buildings. Evidence for burning, moreover, is more likely due to natural carelessness than malicious intent.

These new ideas have been particularly prevalent on Hadrian's Wall and, in this context, two inscriptions from the fort at Birdoswald, now in Tullie House Museum at Carlisle, are of particular significance. One records the restoration of a granary in A.D. 205–8; and the second that of the *praetorium*, or commanding officer's house, which "had been covered with earth and fal-

len into ruin", the *pincipia* and the bath house in A.D. 297–305. The first inscription used to be seen as part of the evidence for reconstruction after trouble with the natives at the end of the second century A.D., and the other for barbarian raids during the usurpation of Carausius or Allectus. Both events are now subject to some scepticism.

Quite apart from these inscriptions, the position and surviving structures of Birdoswald Fort are of considerable interest. Its function was to guard the valley of the River Irthing, which runs from north-east to southwest through the surrounding hills, and the bridge over it at Willowford. The fort was originally built astride the turf wall with the main east and west gates immediately forward of it, as at Chesters. When the Wall, originally of turf, was rebuilt in stone its line was changed to run to the north-east and northwest corners, so negating this arrangement.

As you approach the site today from the

modern road you will first of all see the impressive remains of the fort wall at its north-west corner, standing over 6 feet high. The east gate is also well preserved with the piers of the north portal still standing to full height and the springer stone for the arch in place. The tower over the gate had evidently col-lapsed by the late third century, A.D., further evidence for neglect, and in subsequent res-toration, the north portal was blocked. At the south gate, the east portal was blocked soon after its erection and became a guard cham-ber. In later times, the west portal was closed; look carefully at the east wall of the west portal and you will see rather rough masonry which is taken to be reconstruction of the late fourth century A.D., possibly the work of Count Theodosius in 369 A.D., during the last serious restoration of Britain's defences.
See **Hadrian's Wall, Emperors in Britain.**

Above left, guardroom at the east gate. Top, detail of the south gate, and above, the fort and landscape to the west.

Temples and Religion
Of Gods and Men

When the Roman armies arrived, they not only brought new gods and new religious practices, but they also brought literacy and a tradition of monumental sculpture. Through inscriptions and representations in stone, therefore, we can learn more about the religion of the Britons and the effects of Roman culture on it. In some respects, Roman and native beliefs would have been quite similar; both were based on the commemoration of natural events through the year and the perception of spiritual value in natural phenomena. There are, for example, many Roman dedications to the *genius loci*, or spirit of the place. The Romans also believed in the power of votive offerings, as the mass of objects, especially coins, thrown in the spring at Bath shows, and the presence of an augurer, or *haruspex*, attached to the adjoining temple is proof of indulgence in animal sacrifice.

Religious tolerance was very much a hallmark of the Roman Empire; continuity of sacred sites was allowed and a merging of deities derived from the classical pantheon with native gods possessing similar attributes was common. The union of Mars with Celtic war gods is, for example, known in many parts of Britain including Chedworth where the local deity is named Lenus; Caerwent where he is Ocelus; and in Suffolk where he glories in the name of Corotiacus. An instance of what is known as "syncretism" with official approval is the association of the native Sul with the Roman Minerva as the presiding spirit at Bath.

Other gods were introduced by the Roman army which were not classical in origin, but came from conquered provinces. The cult of the *Matres*, or mothers, although Celtic, seems to have reached Britain from the Rhineland. They are essentially fertility goddesses and can be seen as a triad – a typical Celtic way of expressing special powers – at Cirencester, for example, or, curiously, as a group of four in a relief from London.

In the official world of the army and provincial administration, traditional and formalized religious ceremonies were obligatory. They would have included observation of traditional Roman festivals – such as the Floralia (at the Beginning of May) and the Saturnalia (in mid-December), forerunner of Christmas – and worship of classical deities, especially Jupiter, Juno and Minerva who made up the Capitoline Triad and were seen as guardians of the Roman state. Many military altars have dedications to Jupiter Optimus Maximus, usually abbreviated to I.O.M.

The other important form of state religion involved worship of deceased emperors and of the *numen*, or spirit, of the reigning emperor: "I believe I am becoming a god" are supposed to be the wry last words of Vespasian. Although this cult may have its origins in traditional Roman ancestor worship, it had the clear purpose of unifying a very diverse empire in a spiritual as well as a political sense. The basilica of every Roman town and the *principia* of every fort would, therefore, have had an image of the emperor in the *aedes* and the citizens or the army unit designated priests to perform the required rites. The centre of the imperial cult in Britain was the Temple of Claudius at Colchester.

Outside official duties, men worshipped as they pleased and this explains the numerous temples found near forts, such as that to Antenociticus at Benwell. Tolerance ended, however, where a religion specifically denied the validity of the state's official theology. It was then seen as a political threat and this explains the persecution of the Jews and the Christians.

Christianity was only one of a number of new cults spreading into north-western Europe from the east by the end of the second century A.D. Their adherents sought a more intimate relationship with their gods than that offered by traditional religion, and hoped for some form of salvation or eternal life after death. The convert would first, however, undergo an initiation into the mysteries of the cult which usually involved some form of ordeal leading to divine revelation. Togetherness through communal worship was also a new feature of the spiritual life, and congregations adopted the basilican type of building familiar from the forts and the forum for their churches and temples.

One of the most prominent of these "mystery" religions was Mithraeism. Mithras was a sun deity of Persian origin, especially popular with the army and merchant class. Initiation rites, which included a symbolic rebirth into the light after forced imprisonment in a dark pit, were severe and the martial character of the cult was reinforced by the exclusion of women. The central myth usually commemorated by a relief over the altar was the so-called "tauroctony", in which Mithras, eyes cast heavenwards, sits astride the sacred bull and ritually cuts its throat out of which the blood to create new life gushes liberally forth.

Evidence for Mithraeism's rival, Christianity, is also widespread in Britain; particularly in and around towns which, as centres of trade and communications, were quick to absorb new ideas. Of particular interest are items bearing the chi-rho symbol, the first three letters of Christ's name in Greek, which can be found, for example, on items in the hoard of church plate from Water Newton, the walls of the house church at Lullingstone and on the Hinton St Mary mosaic in the British Museum.

Although Constantine made the Roman Empire officially Christian in A.D. 313, pagan cults survived in the fourth century A.D., especially those, which as numerous villa mosaics show, involved, just as Christianity did, ideas concerning the search for eternal life. Bacchus and Orpheus appear to have been deities with a particular hold on the Romano-British imagination. At a different level, Celtic cults also retained their appeal and offerings were still being thrown into Coventina's well near Carrawburgh fort at the end of the fourth century A.D.. Diversity of belief and practice remained the hallmark of religion in Britain throughout the Roman era.

See **Bath, Benwell, Caernafon, Caerwent, Lincoln, Lullingstone, Silchester.**

HADRIAN'S WALL

Piper Sike, Cumbria

OS 86 NY 588653

The turret is to be found on the north side of the minor road between Banks East and Birdoswald.

Although Hadrian's Wall west of the Irthing was initially built of turf, the turrets, such as that at Piper Sike, continued to be built of stone. It is, perhaps, difficult to imagine a tower some 20 feet high here today when only footings survive, but there is, as at many Wall sites, an excellent Department of the Environment notice with a reconstruction drawing of the site in Roman times. While the troops obviously patrolled their section of Wall from the top of the tower they lived in the groundfloor room and excavation located a hearth in the middle of it.

Piper Sike Turret, like that at Coesike, had evidently become surplus to requirements by the late second century A.D. and was allowed to fall into ruins. Immediately to the north of the turret, the Wall ditch can be clearly seen. *See* **Hadrian's Wall, Hadrian's Wall – Coesike, Hadrian's Wall – Banks East.**

HADRIAN'S WALL

Banks East

Cumbria

OS 86 NY 575647

The site is on a minor road some 5 miles north-east of the village of Brampton on the A69 (9 miles east of Carlisle). Travellers might care to visit picturesque Lanercost Priory while in the area.

This turret is rather better preserved than that at Piper Sike, the next turret but one to the east, and is of particular interest because the plinth at the foot of the walls, typical of turf wall turrets, can be clearly seen. Notice also how the stone wall has been butted up to the turret indicating that the turret is the earlier structure.

The reason for initially building the western section of Hadrian's Wall in turf is unknown, but one suggestion is that the lack of readily available limestone for use in mortar, and about 1 mile west of Banks East there is the so-called Red Rock Fault which marks a change in the surface geology from limestone to sandstone. No limestone occurs near the Wall line from this point westwards. *See* **Hadrian's Wall, Hadrian's Wall – Piper Sike.**

Major excavations in recent years have revealed important evidence for the history of Roman Carlisle. The first fort, founded by Agricola, used the same defensible piece of ground now occupied by the medieval castle. It formed the west end of the Stanegate frontier system and lasted for some fifteen to twenty years. When Hadrian's Wall was constructed a new fort was built at Stanwix north of the River Eden which was the largest on the Wall line and probably served as command H.Q. for the whole garrison. A civilian community began to flourish here in the later second century A.D. and may have become capital of the *civitas* of the Carvetii in the third century A.D.

Although its Roman sequence is long and complex, those in search of visible remains must turn to the Tullie House Museum. The museum has a fine collection of antiquities with many items from the Wall forts and Carlisle itself. You will, for example, see the two inscriptions recording construction work at Birdoswald, but travellers will probably adopt as a particular favourite the well-known tombstone depicting a lady holding a large fan. In view of the usual weather conditions in Cumbria, however, the sculptor's inspiration must have been Mediterranean. Notice also the small child at the woman's knee who has put his pet bird in her lap. The stone is topped by a winged sphinx holding a skull flanked by two lions devouring human heads.

From Carlisle, it is possible to trace the line of Hadrian's Wall westwards to a fort at Bowness-on-Solway. A system of control with mile fortlets and towers was then extended along the Cumbrian coast to a fort at Maryport and on to St Bees Head. The remains in these areas are, however, not striking.
See **Hadrian's Wall, Hadrian's Wall – Birdoswald.**

HADRIAN'S WALL
Carlisle
(Luguvalium)
Cumbria
OS 85 NY 400560
The city of Carlisle is 307 miles north of London. By road, it is reached by the M1 and M6; by train from Euston Station, London. Although the Roman interest is confined to the Tullie House Museum, there is a fine medieval castle and a cathedral neither of which should be missed.

HARDKNOTT

(Mediobogdum)

Cumbria

OS 90 NY 218015

The fort lies on a minor road running from the A595 near Ravenglass to the A593 near Ambleside. Hardknott Pass and, to the east of it, Wrynose Pass are very steep and can be extremely hazardous in poor weather.

Above right, footings of the north angle-tower, far right, the valley of the River Esk below the fort. Below right, the approach to the site by road from the east via Wrynose and Hardknott Passes has gradients of 1:3 and is recommended to only the most intrepid of motorists, whereas access to the site from the west makes no such demands. Below, far right, walls and butresses.

96

The Roman fort on Hardknott pass cannot fail to stir the imagination. Because the walls survive so well and because the rugged and dramatic surroundings are so unspoilt, it takes little effort to picture Hardknott (Mediobogdum) when it was one of the more remote outposts of the army guarding the fortress road through Eskdale. Spare a thought, however, for the 500 men of the Fourth Cohort of Dalmations from Yugoslavia, for in winter the weather is a harsh mistress.

The history of the fort is quite simple: it was one of a series established in the Lake District to consolidate Roman presence in an area initially conquered by Agricola on his march north to Scotland. According to inscriptions, it was founded during Hadrian's reign and is at the mid-point, as the Latin name suggests, on a road from Ravenglass to Ambleside – a place where the weary traveller might take welcome rest and change his horses or mules. In case of trouble from local tribesmen, however, the strategic position is excellent with a precipitous drop away from the fort walls on their north and west sides.

These walls still survive to a height of 6 feet. At each corner, there is a turret or watch tower which you should note have no doorway at ground level showing that they were entered instead at rampart walkway level. Within the fort, there are the remains of the *principia*, flanked on one side by two granaries, which have the typical buttresses supporting the walls and loading platforms at the front, and on the other by the commanding officer's house. The poor fellow seems, however, to have enjoyed rather less spacious quarters than he may have expected, for only the north wing was built even by the time the fort was abandoned in the late second century A.D.

Two features outside the fort walls should now command your attention. There is a bath house by the south gate showing that even, or perhaps especially, in these wild parts the soldiers demanded traditional comforts. In winter it was probably the only warm place. Secondly, there is a deliberately flattened area forming the parade ground some 250 yards to the north-east. This is a remarkable survival, unique in Britain, although every military base would originally have had one. Discipline and training were at the heart of the Roman army's success and a high standard was expected of the men wherever they might be. The romantic will doubtless stand on the natural knoll used here as the commander's *tribunal* and shout orders to ghostly troops drawn up below, but they will not be the first to be moved by the image of the place described in the poetry of Wordsworth as:

. . . that lone Camp on Hardknott's height,
Whose guardians bent the knee to Jove and
    Mars.

See **The Army, Bath Houses.**

Villas
Down on the Farm

The remains of the great villas, such as Bignor, Chedworth and Lulling-stone, are among the most exciting and evocative monuments to the Roman occupation of Britain. Villa owners would have been among the very highest echelons of contemporary society. In some cases, they might be government employees but usually they were Britons who, through official sponsorship or personal enterprise, had the wealth to acquire land, the safest form of investment in the ancient world, and to adopt Roman culture and customs. By the early fourth century A.D., such men were, judging by the themes depicted on their mosaic pavements, familiar with classical literature and mythology and indulged in serious philosophical and religious speculation.

Strictly speaking, the word "villa" means a farm but in the Mediter-ranean world, a villa owner would spend much of his time, as all civilized people did, in town – leaving the villa as more of a country seat. In Britain, with no urban tradition, a villa has rather different economic and social implications. The villas usually grew slowly from native farms, gradually acquiring features influenced by Romanized architectural ideas, includ-ing stone walls, multiple rooms, hypocausts, mosaics and bath houses, while their owners remained rurally based. The palace at Fishbourne may have had some influence, in an artistic and architectural sense, on those who saw it but since it had no farm attached, it cannot be directly compared with other villas in Britain, which were dependent on their agricultural estates for income.

The majority of the villas which we see today are in their late third or fourth centuries A.D. form and are the result of additions made over many years. There were some lavish early villas in Britain, including the so-called government official's house at Lullingstone, but in the first and second centuries A.D. they more usually consist of a single range of rooms, and hypocausts, mosaics and bath houses are rare. The impres-sion created is that all the inhabitants lived more or less together as a single social unit. As time went on, however, a corridor might be added so that the rooms need no longer be used as passages, and wings were built at the ends of the building for extra accommodation. The "winged-corridor" house would permit extra privacy for some inhabitants and allow a certain social differentiation to be emphasized between the owner and his staff. Another innovation was the bath house, at first isolated as a separate structure to minimize the risk of a fire spreading. Finally, in the later third and early fourth centuries A.D., there was a "golden age" of villa construction. Pre-existing buildings were revamped and new ones constructed, on occasions perhaps with second storeys. A common plan at this time was of three substantial wings around a courtyard. Bath houses became a necessity and were usually united with the rest of the building.

The farm was never far away, however, and farm buildings and work-shops were frequently to be found in the main courtyard, as they were at Rockbourne, for example. Villa locations are, perhaps, the best indication of their place in the economy. They are, first of all, concentrated in the areas of richer agricultural land in the south and east of England; there are few north of the Humber, except in the fertile vales of east Yorkshire. Secondly, villas tend to cluster along routes of communication, especially roads and, thirdly, they are rarely far from towns since they made their living by selling agricultural produce in urban markets, where manufactured and imported luxury goods could be purchased in exchange. There are, therefore, particular concentrations around Cirencester, Dorchester and Ilchester (Somerset). The fortunes of Britain's villas seem, in fact, closely tied to that of the towns, with growth in the late first and second centuries A.D. as urbanization took off and further growth during the urban resurgence in the early fourth century A.D. when both Cirencester and Dorchester were able to support specialist mosaic workshops which served the villas in their hinterland.

Villas may have depended on farming, but it is difficult to reconstruct the details of their agricultural regime. It is, for example, not known how large their estates were, although it has been suggested, on the basis of detailed research, that Bignor owned about 2,000 acres. There is also some debate as to whether the Romans really brought any improvements in agricultural technology. A plough suitable for working heavy clay soils, as opposed to the lighter chalk and limestone soils exploited throughout most of prehistory, was available to the late Iron Age farmer and the model of a plough team from Piercebridge, which shows a plough with no wheels or mould board to turn the sod, suggests little change in the Roman period. It would seem, however, that, as part of the empire, Britain was linked to a more dynamic economic system and was, therefore, farmed more intensively. The export trade in grain coupled with the demands of the army brought a great deal of new capital into farming. Roads opened up the countryside and gave farmers ready access to the new urban markets. New land was brought into cultivation and its owners became rich men.

After the mid-fourth century A.D., towns began to decline and, although there are mosaics and other improvements to villa buildings which can be dated to the last years of the century, the great period of growth was over. With increasing marketing difficulties and worsening communications, villas were forced to become more self-sufficient. There is evidence for living rooms being turned over to agricultural purposes and corn-drying kilns were dug into mosaic floors. The date of final desertion is usually difficult to determine but, in many cases, some sort of occupation must have continued into the fifth century A.D., after which the estates, but not the buildings, must have been taken over and farmed again in their own way by the Anglo-Saxon newcomers.

See **Bignor, Chedworth, Fishbourne, North Leigh, Rockbourne.**

HIGH ROCHESTER

(Bremenium)
Northumberland
OS 80 NY 833986

The Village of Rochester is 37 miles north-east of Newcastle and 21 south-east of Jedburgh on the A68. To visit the fort, take the minor road at the south end of the village. You will find two farms within the fort; it is courteous to ask for permission to look at the gates.

If you drive north from Corbridge on the A68 you will follow the line of Dere Street, the great Roman road to the north, for much of the way. A few miles south of the village of Rochester, however, you may notice that where the modern road turns north-east to cross the River Rede and join the A696, the Roman road goes straight on and continues to run almost straight towards the east gate of the fort at High Rochester. The word "High" is appropriate here as the fort's situation is a striking one, commanding the valley of the Rede to the west and that of one of its tributaries to the north; this may be the "roaring stream" which is how the Roman name is translated. Recent farm buildings occupy the site, but the defences can still be traced around most of their circuit.

The first fort was established here by Agricola during his campaigns in the north, but was abandoned in about A.D. 100. The site was reoccupied with the great move north to the Antonine Wall and formed part of the defensive system controlling the Scottish Lowlands. In the early third century A.D., the Emperor Severus initiated further work here when he revived Roman ambitions in Scotland. The third-century A.D. garrison was the First Cohort of Loyal Vardullians and a tombstone of one of their officers, Rufinus, can be seen in the church porch. During his career, he had also been a public official in Rome and his wife was evidently high born. One cannot help wondering what they made of this bleak outpost. Also among the garrison at this time was a detachment of *exploratores*, or scouts, and this explains High Rochester's role as a forward station for the frontier on Hadrian's Wall.

The remains visible today are largely the work of Severus or Constantius, almost a century later. Pride of place must go to the west gate where you can see the northern pier with a splendid moulded capital and springer stone for the arch still surviving. A few stones belonging to the *porta praetoria*, or north gate, can also be seen and there is other stonework elsewhere.

The fort was abandoned in the mid-fourth century A.D., probably at the same time as that at Risingham, 8½ miles to the south, where prominent earthworks can also be seen.

Finally, the intrepid traveller to High Rochester should be able to find the stone base of a circular tomb on the line of Dere Street about half a mile south-west of the fort. *See* **Hadrian's Wall.**

Opposite page, the west gate, its moulded capital and springer stone. Left, the site announces itself to the visitor, in Latin.

One of the most evocative ancient sites in Britain is Hod Hill. In origin an Iron Age hill-fort, it was probably one of the tribal centres of the Durotriges reduced by Vespasian and the Second Augustan Legion on their drive to the south-west after the invasion in A.D. 43. Indeed, excavations here found evidence for bombardment with large military catapults, or *ballistae*. After the natives had capitulated, a Roman fort was constructed in the north-west corner of the enclosure reusing its defences on the north and west sides. On the other two sides, the Roman defences consisted of an inner rampart and two "punic" ditches with a platform between them as at camp D at Cawthorn. The ditch shape makes them more difficult to get out of than to get into, and their spacing means defenders were less vulnerable to hand-thrown missiles while being able themselves to direct devastating fire from the ramparts. The fort entrances to the south and east are also cunningly designed to narrow inwards. Men attempting a frontal assault on the gate would find themselves jostling each other as they approached it with some of their number probably falling in the ditches.

Complete excavation of the fort located slots for timber buildings, and so revealed the most complete plan known for an invasion period fort in Britain which may, perhaps, have accommodated some 600 legionaries and 250 auxiliaries. The fort was abandoned in about A.D. 52 or 53 when the tense atmosphere surrounding the pacification of the Durotriges had presumably passed. There are similar forts of the period on nearby Ham Hill and Waddon Hill.
See **Cawthorn, Maiden Castle, Native Background, The Army.**

HOD HILL Dorset
OS 194 ST 855106
The fort is about 3¼ miles north-west of Blandford Forum. Take the A350 to the village of Stourpaine, then turn left at the pub, and then first right. Keep going until you reach a stream and walk up the track to the south-east corner of the fort. If you are interested in hillforts, be sure to visit Hambledon Hill 2 miles or so to the north-west.

INCHTUTHIL

Tayside
OS 53 NO 125396

To reach the fortress, take the A93 north from Perth until you reach the A984. Turn left here and continue along the A984 until you come to the B947 to Blairgowrie on the right. Opposite the junction is a track. Unless you have a Landrover, you should park on the main road and walk. It is about 1¼ miles to the site. Go to the river, turn right, and when you reach some cottages keep right and go through the fieldgate.

"The third year of Agricola's campaigns brought him into contact with fresh peoples, for the territory of tribes was ravaged as far north as the estuary called the Tay." This is how Tacitus introduces the campaigns of his famous father-in-law in A.D. 80 or 81 when the Romans first took a serious interest in Scotland. Three years later, Tacitus reports: "In the summer in which his sixth year of office began, Agricola enveloped the tribes beyond the Forth."

It was this campaign that led to the foundation of a new legionary fortress at Inchtuthil. When you stand in the middle of the site surrounded by the peaceful countryside of Perthshire, it is worth considering that had Agricola's plans for Scottish conquest gone ahead as planned, you might now be in a bustling city like, for example, York where a fortress had been founded only a few years earlier.

Agricola's successor as governor, whose name is not known for certain, probably intended to continue his work in the north, but because Britain had to lose a legion to meet trouble on the Rhineland, the Scottish conquests, along with the Inchtuthil Fortress, had to be abandoned incomplete, probably in A.D. 86, never to be reoccupied.

It is, however, rare to be able to visit a Roman site which was, without much doubt,

personally chosen by one of the great figures of imperial history. As you approach the site, you will see how it lies on a low promontory above the River Tay with communications, water supply and defence in mind. Because the site has remained open since Roman times, large-scale excavations have been possible here and, uniquely, the complete plan of the fortress has been recovered. Since the internal buildings were timber and, moreover, systematically dismantled by the army, no trace remains but you can still follow the defences. Originally, they consisted of a ditch and turf rampart but it was soon given a stone wall, making Inchtuthil the first fortress in Britain to be defended in this way. This suggests that it was envisaged as a permanent base of the conquest of Scotland. The most prominent feature of the defences today is on their south-west side, where a stretch of rampart still stands several feet high.

To the south-west of the fortress, three temporary camps are known which probably housed the soldiers during construction work on the fortress itself, but the only earthwork to be seen here is the so-called "Western Vallum", a bank and ditch running north-west to south-east and forming an extra defence across the western end of the promontory. *See* **The Army.**

KINGSTON UPON HULL

North Humberside
OS 107 TA 100290

Kingston upon Hull is 215 miles north from London and reached by way of the M1, A1 and M62.

Hull has no Roman post itself; the nearest substantial Roman settlement was at Brough on Humber (Petuaria) some 10 miles to the west, but the Museum of Transport and Archaeology is a must for all Romanists.

The great feature of the museum is a collection of fourth-century A.D. mosaics from villas at Brantingham and Rudston in east Yorkshire and Horkstow in Lincolnshire. The principal Brantingham mosaic is known as the Tyche mosaic. Tyche was originally a Goddess of Fortune, but is often used as a divine personification of a province or city, hence the crown in the mosaic's central figure which represents a stylized city wall.

The Rudston mosaics include one, from the villa bath suite, which appropriately depicts sea monsters. Another has a naïve and, depending on your point of view, crude or charming representation of the Goddess

Venus. She is identified, firstly, by the apple in her right hand – won in the famous beauty contest with Juno and Athena, thanks to the judgement of Paris of Troy – and, secondly, by the mirror which in this case looks more like a frying pan. The great beauty's body is also sadly distorted. Below her is a merman, or triton, holding a torch. Around the central scene are four animal panels; although the leopard is more like a domestic cat, you will enjoy the bull referred to in an inscription as "omacida" or man-killing. Compare this mosaic with the equally naïve wolf and twins from Aldborough in Leeds Museum.

The Horkstow mosaics include a partial panel depicting Orpheus who, as usual, is charming the beasts with his magic lyre. Another panel from the same pavement shows a chariot race. *See* **Malton, Villas.**

LINCOLN

(Lindum)
Lincolnshire
OS 121 SK 970710

The city is 141 miles north of London and can be reached by way of the A1 and A46 through Newark. Lincoln is one of the most attractive historic towns in Britain; be sure to visit the cathedral and the unique Norman stone houses on Steep Hill.

A good place to start a tour of Roman Lincoln is on top of the aptly named Observatory Tower in the south-east corner of the medieval castle. From here, you will immediately appreciate the all-important topographical situation which has determined the pattern of settlement in the city since, perhaps, the late 50s when a fortress was constructed here by the Ninth Legion at the end of a spur of high ground, the Lincoln Edge, overlooking the River Witham and commanding views

over a wide area to the south.

The fortress appears to have replaced an even earlier military base in the river valley at the point where Ermine Street, coming up from the south, and the Fosse Way, coming from the south-west, meet. There is a known legionary cemetery in this area and the tombstones of Gaius Valerius, a standard bearer, and Gaius Saufeius, an ordinary soldier, now to be seen in the museum probably date before A.D. 50 because their names lack the usual third element, or *cognomen*, that Roman citizens employed from the later first century A.D. onwards.

Lincoln is of particular interest because of the sequence of its defences, and work of most of the major periods of construction can still be seen above ground reflecting the changing requirements of the whole Roman era.

The first fortress defences consisted of a ditch and earthen bank, box-like in cross-section since it was revetted back and front in timber. This is unusual in Britain, but presumably turf for the creation of the usual rampart of this period with a sloping front and rear was unavailable. Timber towers completed the work.

Between about A.D. 85 and 95, the fortress was converted into one of Britain's early *coloniae*, or settlements for retired legionaries. The colonists reused the legionary defences, and in the early second century A.D. refurbished them with a stone wall, a section of which can be seen in East Bight near the north gate, known as the Newport Arch. At one point, it had what was thought to be a water tank built behind it. In the mid-to-late second century A.D., stone interval towers were added to the defences and the base of one of them can also be seen here.

The Newport Arch consists of the inner arch of a barrel-vaulted gateway – the outer arch has long since gone – and two smaller side passages flanked by guard chambers with semi-circular outer faces. It probably dates to the third century A.D. This is one of the best surviving Roman town gates in Britain, although it had to be heavily restored a few years ago after being hit by a refrigerator truck. Remember also that Roman ground level is about 6 feet below the modern street, so the imposing nature of the arch is not apparent since its "feet" are deeply buried.

If you now follow the line of the defences around towards the east gate, you will eventually find a fine stretch of Roman wall standing up to 14 feet high above the modern ground level in the grounds of the Eastgate Hotel. In front of the hotel is the east gate itself. It had a single main portal, like the Newport Arch with which it is probably contemporary, and towers on either side, again with semi-circular faces. The base of the north tower is preserved and you can also see the positions of posts for an earlier timber gate marked out.

From the east gate return to Bailgate, the main north-south street and notice the stone settings in the pavement which mark the location of column bases for the *colonia*'s forum colonnade. Two bases survive *in situ* in a nearby cellar. The forum reused the site of the legionary *principia*. The basilica was on the north side of the courtyard and part of its rear wall still survives as the so-called Mint Wall, the only upstanding piece of forum wall in Britain. Close by you can also see the unusual tiled arches of a well head discovered in excavation of the forum's east range.

An even more remarkable discovery in the courtyard of the forum was a Roman church. This small apsed building, now marked out on the modern ground surface, may well have been the seat of the Bishop of Lincoln, named Adelfius, sent along with two others from Britain to the Council of Arles in A.D. 314. Although there may have been a brief relapse into paganism before the mission of Paulinus in the early seventh century A.D., this small building can fairly be seen as ancestor to Lincoln's great cathedral.

If you now make your way down Steep Hill, you will find yourself in the "lower town". As you might expect, settlement in the form of shops and craftsmen's booths, or *canabae*, grew up here soon after the fortress was established; some of the local people obviously had an eye for the business which 6,000 legionaries might put their way. By the end of the second century A.D., the lower town was evidently a flourishing settlement sufficiently important to warrant its own defences. They initially consisted of a stone wall with a rampart and ditch; interval towers were added in the third century A.D.

The lower town wall can be seen near the Bishop's Palace, but of greater interest is part exposed at The Park near the south-west corner. Here a gate was inserted at some stage after the interval towers had been added and, in the fourth century A.D., it was upgraded with rectangular towers which reused a number of elaborate architectural fragments. Finally, perhaps during Theodosius's restoration of British defences after the "Barbarian Conspiracy", the wall was rebuilt north of the gate and thickened to the south of it.
See **The Army, Towns.**

In the early eighteenth century, a mosaic was discovered in the grounds of the great Tudor country house at Littlecote which was acclaimed to be, ". . . the finest pavement that the sun ever shone upon in England". It has recently been rediscovered and restored and its bright colours and mysterious designs once again impress the visitor.

The mosaic lies in two rooms at the north-west corner of the villa whose purpose is, at present, the subject of some debate. One room is rectangular, but the other to the south-west, has a most unusual form known as a "triconch", meaning that it has three apses. In the first room, the mosaic is largely geometric, but greatest interest attaches to the floor in the apsed room as this holds the key to the villa owner's intellectual interests and the function of the building itself.

The central figure plays a lyre and is accompanied by a canine animal, either a dog or a fox. We may have a representation

LITTLECOTE
Wiltshire
OS 174 SU 301705
The villa is in the grounds of Littlecote House, 2½ miles north-west of Hungerford (Berkshire) off the A419.

of Apollo here or, alternatively, Orpheus, or even some cryptic mixture of the two. In any case, we seem to be in a similar world of metaphysical speculation to that which the traveller will encounter at Bignor and Brading. The allusions here are again to the search for salvation and eternal life through the discovery of secret knowledge induced by intense spiritual experience.

Around the central roundel, there are four

the Littlecote building is of this period. You should notice, however, that the putative temple was only one part of a larger structure, converted from an ordinary agricultural barn. There is also a small bath suite where, perhaps, religious ceremonies akin to baptism took place.

See **Bignor, Brading, Chedworth, Temples and Religion, Villas.**

Clearly labelled footings, skillfully restored mosaics, and a well presented site museum make Littlecote Roman Villa an excellent starting point for newcomers to the delights of discovering Roman Britain.

female figures with accompanying beasts who represent the eternal cycle of birth to death through the allegory of the four seasons – another common motif of mosaics of this period. Aphrodite (Venus), represents birth and spring; Nemesis, youth and summer; Demeter (Ceres), maturity and autumn; and Persephone, death and winter. The purpose of the animals is unclear, but may suggest the transformations which the god Dionysus underwent to escape from would-be assassins. In the apses, the sun's rays radiate from an animal's face; the pursuit of spiritual light is presumably the theme here.

The overall impression created by the mosaics and the rooms in which they lie, is of a temple and it is worth bearing in mind that churches in the Byzantine world frequently have a very similar plan. We know, moreover, that paganism continued to flourish in fourth-century A.D. Britain in spite of Christianity's official status. Indeed, during the reign of the Emperor Julian (A.D. 361–3), paganism was reinstated and it is possible that

The role of London (Londinium) in the early years of the Roman occupation is not altogether clear but, at present, there is little evidence for a fort here. A river crossing must have been established, however, at the time of the invasion and the attractions of the site as a natural centre for communications by land and water soon became apparent. Colchester may claim to be Britain's first capital, but it was soon supplanted by London.

Urban planning probably began in the 50s with streets laid out over what were then two low hills either side of the vally of the Walbrook. The course of this stream is still preserved in a street name near the Bank of England which, incidentally, incorporates, an eighteenth-century copy of the Temple of Vesta at Tivoli near Rome. Excavations in the stream bed have produced a number of human skulls which may be grim testimony to the revolt of Boudicca in A.D. 60, who destroyed London along with Colchester and St Albans.

By the 80s, London had recovered sufficiently to have its first forum built and there is also evidence for the construction of a large palace belonging to the provincial governor on a terraced site overlooking the Thames. In addition to a large staff of civil servants, the governor had a personal guard of 1,000 soldiers, known as *singulares*, and during the reign of the Emperor Hadrian (A.D. 117–38), a fort was built in the Cripplegate area to house them. The forum was also rebuilt on a massive scale at this time.

London's prosperity in the first and second centuries A.D. was probably founded on commerce – a strong element of which was trade with northern Europe. Britain's minerals and agricultural products were exported and luxury goods, such as wine, spices and high-quality metal work, were imported for redistribution around the country. It is not surprising, therefore, that extensive quays have been found in the Thames Street area. It is worth noting also that the river was considerably wider in Roman times, with the north bank in the first century A.D. being roughly where the north side of Thames Street is today. Since then, land reclamation has moved the bank some 300 feet further south.

In about A.D. 200, Roman London was surrounded by a wall with a rampart behind it and a ditch in front of it; parts of it amazingly still survive, partly because the medieval city walls followed the same line. In the third century A.D., however, London seems to have stagnated, even declined in terms of prosperity and population, perhaps due to changes in the imperial economy brought about by political upsets which reduced the scale of long-distance trade. The isolation of Britain during the usurpation of Carausius and Allectus must have been particularly damaging. No wonder the citizens of London rejoiced when, as he claims on a special commemorative medal, Constantius Chlorus restored the "eternal light" in A.D. 296.

There are signs of a revival in the early fourth century A.D. when London became the seat of the *vicarius* of Britain, that is, the official who oversaw the four provinces into which the country had now been divided. London was also capital of one of these provinces and was apparently now known as Augusta.

The revival was short-lived as the political situation deteriorated. To combat the threat of barbarian raids up the Thames, bastions were added to the wall on its east side and, in the second half of the fourth century A.D., a riverside wall was built. This obviously meant blocking off the quays, but security had to come first. The wall contained a lot of reused stone, including tombstones and pieces of a free-standing monumental arch which can now be seen in the Museum of London. The last attempt to defend Roman London was probably undertaken by the Vandal general, Stilicho, at the very end of the fourth century A.D. and a stretch of wall at the Tower of London may be his work.

Aspects of Roman London may still be seen at the following sites.

See **Emperors in Britain, Towns.**

LONDON
OS 177 TQ400800
The nation's capital with good road and rail links to most major provincial centres. London, of course, has potent historical associations with all periods of British history, but travellers visiting the City, where the Roman remains are concentrated, may also be interested in visiting the Tower of London, St Paul's Cathedral and other famous churches designed by Sir Christopher Wren after the great fire of 1666.

Note that finding the sites in this guide will be made all the easier by acquiring the O.S. Map of Londinium (Roman London) on sale at the Museum of London and elsewhere.

Following excavation after the Second World War blitz, the south-west corner and part of the west side of the Cripplegate fort wall were exposed, along with the remains of the corner tower and interval tower. Butting up to the fort wall at the corner is the later town wall. There is also evidence in places here for contemporary strengthening of the inner face of the fort wall.

LONDON Noble Street EC2
OS 177 TQ 322815
The nearest Underground station is St Pauls, from where you should walk up St Martin's le Grand, turn right into Gresham Street, and Noble Street is first left.

In an inspection chamber off London Wall, you can see the remains of a guardroom belonging to the west gate of the fort and a piece of fort wall. (Note this site is not open to the public on a regular basis.)

LONDON Bastion House EC2
OS 177 TQ 322816
This is in London Wall. The nearest Underground station is St Pauls or Barbican.

LONDON St Alphage's
Churchyard EC2
OS 177 TQ 323816
The churchyard is in St Alphage
Garden off London Wall. Take the
Underground to Barbican or
St Pauls.

Dwarfed now by the new Barbican development, there is a section of city wall here of many periods. It survives to the height it was in the fifteenth century. Much of the core, at least in the lower half, may be Roman but the

facing is medieval. If, however, you look at the base of the wall on its outer face, you can just see the Roman fort wall and the later thickening again.

LONDON Dukes Place EC3
OS 177 TQ 335815
The subway is close to Aldgate
Underground station.

A curiosity in the display of Roman London but an informative one, none the less, is to be found at Dukes Place as a result of excavation in advance of the construction of a new subway. The city wall was breached and a sim-

plified cross-section showing the main features found – plinth, rubble core, tile courses and rampart – have been picked out in coloured tiles on the subway wall.

LONDON Cooper's Row EC3
OS 177 TQ 337810
Take the Underground to Tower
Hill. Cooper's Row is the street
running north towards Fenchurch
Street Station. The Roman wall is in
an open area on the right-hand
side.

All the main features of the Roman wall are visible here. At the base of its outer face is the red sandstone plinth. The main body of the wall is built of courses of Kentish ragstone

facing a mortared rubble core. At intervals, there are courses of tiles which bond the faces together and give the wall extra stability.

LONDON Tower Hill EC3
OS 177 TQ 336807
Take the Underground to Tower
Hill.

The ragstone facing and tile-bonding courses can be seen again here in a fine stretch of wall of which the upper part is medieval. Note also a replica of the tombstone of procurator

Julius Classicianus – the original fragments are in the British Museum – and a replica of a bronze statue of Hadrian.

LONDON
Tower of London EC3
OS 177 TQ 335805
Take the Underground to Tower
Hill.

The medieval fortress lies partly within and partly outside the south-east corner of the Roman walled area. This has resulted in the Roman wall itself being largely demolished, apart from one fragment and the base of a fourth-century A.D. bastion which can be seen near William the Conqueror's White Tower.

Of much greater interest is a stretch of east-west wall in the south-east corner of the Tower bailey which may date to as late as the 390s and be the work of Flavius Stilicho during his last desperate attempt to defend the Roman capital.

LONDON
Temple of Mithras EC4
OS 177 TQ 317817
The building is now in Queen
Victoria Street, near Bank
Underground station.

Most of the Mithrea known from Britain are from military sites, such as Caernafon or Carrawburgh, but the cult of Mithras also appealed to merchants, especially, perhaps, to those who had travelled to the east, so it was no surprise to find a temple to the god in London. The building is not now in its original position, since it was found on the banks of the Walbrook stream and moved to its present site after excavation, but its plan is instructive, as it is an apsed basilica, typical

of those required for the "congregationalist" religions, including Christianity, of the later Roman times. Its identification as a Mithraeum was confirmed by the discovery of some remarkable sculpture now to be seen in the Museum of London. They were apparently hidden when the temple was desecrated, probably by Christians, in the late third or early fourth centuries A.D.
See **Temples and Religion.**

LONDON
Museum of London EC4
OS 177 TQ 323818
Take the Underground to Barbican
or St Pauls and follow the signs.

The Museum of London has one of the most imaginative displays of Roman material in Britain. Of particular interest are some of the sculptured stones found reused in the fourth century A.D. riverside wall which came from a free-standing monumental arch decorated with figures of gods, including Minerva and Hercules in relief. More sophisticated stone carving is represented by the statuary from

the Temple of Mithras. Look out for a great marble head of Mithras who wears a Greek Phrygian cap and has his eyes rolled characteristically skywards. The tauroctony, or bull-slaying scene, is also on display along with another marble head, this time of the eastern god Serapis who, according to the myth, was slain by the devil Seth and then restored to life by his wife, Isis.

The outstanding Romano-British collections of the British Museum have recently been splendidly redisplayed and many objects referred to elsewhere in this guide can now be seen to advantage here, including the Water Newton hoard, the Ribchester cavalry parade helmet and the model of a plough team from Piercebridge. Look out also for the Mildenhall treasure from Suffolk, but probably of eastern origin. It is a collection of silver tableware, including the so-called Great Dish which is 2 feet across. The vessels depict scenes of revelry associated with the cult of

Bacchus and show, like a number of mosaics from Britain, the continued popularity of pagan "mystery" cults in the fourth century A.D., when more restrained Christian values were supposedly in the ascendant.

At the top of the main stairs to the first floor of the Museum you will also see the famous Hinton St Mary Mosaic, which has the head of Christ against a background of the chi-rho in the centre and a representation of Bellerophon slaying the mythical beast known as the Chimera at one end.

LONDON
British Museum WC1
OS 177 TQ 304819
Take the Underground to Tottenham Court Road and the Museum is in Great Russell Street – a 5-minute walk.

The importance of religion in the life of the people of Roman Britain can never be underestimated, although evidence for the details of their beliefs largely derives from buildings and monuments associated with the upper classes. Lullingstone is one of a small group of villas which are of vital importance in this respect, since throughout its existence we can trace changing aspects of the spiritual side of men's lives, often ignored in archaeology's more mundane preoccupations with settlement patterns and building details. The culmination of religious activity at the villa was the establishment of one of the earliest Christian shrines in Britain.

In the late first and second century A.D., the site was occupied by a simple farm, the inhabitants of which worshipped in a small circular temple west of the house; sacred, perhaps, to some local Celtic deity. In the last decades of the second century A.D., however, the shrine was abruptly abandoned and the whole status of the buildings was upgraded in a style indicating a newcomer of highly Romanized, even Mediterranean, tastes, who it has been suggested was not a farmer but a government official.

A sunken stone room, now known as the Deep Room, was made into a shrine, or Nymphaeum, as we may call it on the basis of a painting in a wall niche showing three water spirits, perhaps personifications of the nearby River Darenth. The central figure is best preserved; notice the water coming from her nipples. Two marble busts, of which casts can be seen at the site today, would also have adorned the house at this time and were probably revered as embodying the spirit of family ancestors.

After desertion in about A.D. 200, the villa lay empty until the late third century A.D., when it was reconstructed. The discovery of a granary shows that it returned to being a farm, and a wealthy one at that, for in the fourth century A.D. fine mosaics were laid in two rooms which formed the focal point of the house.

In the apsed *triclinium*, or dining room, there is the famous scene showing Europa being abducted and carried out to sea by Jupiter disguised as a white bull. Above it is

an inscription referring to a passage in Virgil's *Aeneid* which translated means: "If jealous Juno had seen thus the swimming of the bull she would with greater justice have repaired to the halls of Aeolus."

The point being that Aeolus, God of the Winds, could have raised a storm to discomfort the adulterer. There need be no particular religious significance in this and dinner guests would have enjoyed the literary allusion, but the mosaic in the second room may introduce a rather different mood. It shows the winged Pegasus ridden by Bellerophon, who is thrusting his lance into the Chimera – a mythical animal, part serpent, part goat, part lion. Around the central panel are representations of the seaons; Spring with a swallow on her shoulder is particularly attractive. It has been suggested that the mosaic is essentially an allegory of "good" triumphing over "evil", – a theme which assumes new meaning in view of the villa's subsequent Christianity since Bellerophon is associated with the specifically Christian mosaic from Hinton St Mary, Dorset, now in the British Museum.

Another building dating to the early years of the villa's reconstruction is the so-called Temple-Mausoleum. Here, a sunken chamber contained two burials: one, in a lead coffin, of a young man; and the other, much disturbed, of a young woman, accompanied by grave goods including a set of gaming counters, glass, bronze and pottery vessels. Above the chamber was a temple of the usual Romano-Celtic type.

In the late fourth century A.D., the inhabitants of the villa became Christian and while the Temple-Mausoleum was allowed to decay, a room decorated with Christian symbols and praying figures was created as a house chapel for the owner's family and, perhaps, close friends. Pagan rituals continued as well, however, as libations were evidently still made to *manes*, or spirits of the dead, of the marble busts in the Deep Room. Eclecticism remained a feature of Roman religion throughout.

See **London – British Museum, Temples and Religion, Villas.**

LULLINGSTONE
OS 177 TQ 530650
The villa is near the village of Eynsford, a few miles east of Bromley.

LYMPNE

(Portus Lemanis)
OS 189 TR 119342

*Lympne village is about 10 miles
west of Folkestone via the A259,
A261 and B2067. From the village
take a footpath south towards the
Royal Military Canal which runs
south of the site.*

All around the coast of Britain, and especially where it is close to the Continent, travellers will see the remains of military emplacements designed to keep seaborne invaders from these shores. "Britons, never, never, never shall be slaves". as the song says.

The late Roman "Saxon Shore" forts are, perhaps, the earliest substantial remains of our coastal defences, but they are only the first in a long line stretching onwards to medieval castles, sometimes on the same site as the Roman forts; Martello towers, to guard against Napoleon; Second World War pill boxes; and sophisticated radar monitoring stations.

As military technology changes, old defensive works naturally fall into ruins and few can be in a greater state of ruin today than the fort at Lympne, or Stutfall Castle, as it is known. Now relatively isolated, but pleasantly picturesque, travellers will also note that it is some way from the sea, but this is due to changes in the coastline since Roman times when it occupied a strategic position overlooking the mouth of a river a little to the east.

In the second century A.D., there was probably a base for the British fleet here and an altar erected, appropriately, to Neptune by Aufidius Pantera, a *praefectus*, or commander of the fleet, was found reused in a later wall. The Saxon Shore fort itself was built in the later third century A.D. and was originally rectangular, with bastions around it, somewhat similar to Richborough, with which it is broadly contemporary, although this is not readily apparent today as the ground has been heavily disturbed by natural slippage. In the *Notitia Dignitatum*, the garrison is listed as the numerous Turnacensium, but since the fort is thought to have been abandoned in the mid-fourth century A.D., it is not immediately apparent why troops were recorded here in the late fourth century.

See **Burgh Castle, Richborough.**

The Romano-Celtic temple on Maiden Castle, now freed by English Heritage from the wrought iron cage that held it for so long.

MAIDEN CASTLE

Dorset
OS 194 SY 670884

*Maiden Castle is just south of
Dorchester. Take the A354
Weymouth Road and there is a sign
marking a turning to the right. You
will find a car park at the base of the
fort.*

One of the most famous finds from Roman Britain is an iron *ballista* bolt lodged in the spine of a man buried in the "war cemetery" outside the east gate of Maiden Castle. As the archaeologist Sir Mortimer Wheeler showed, it is an extraordinary piece of evidence for the ferocious attack on the hillfort by Vespasian's Second Legion. The Romans' opponents of the day were the local Durotrigian tribesmen, such tough and awkward customers that according to Suetonius, as many as twenty of their *oppida*, or fortified places, had to be taken before they yielded.

The defences of Maiden Castle, which you see today, are the product of 2,000 years or so of fortifications and the multiple ditches guarding the east and west gates must have seemed impregnable to the natives. The Roman army knew otherwise, however, and while the artillery strafed the ramparts, other legionaries would have formed the famous *testudo*, or tortoise, holding their shields over their heads for protection while steadily advancing on the fort's most vulnerable point, its double gates.

In the aftermath of defeat, the Britons were left to bury their dead which they did with due ceremony, as pots and joints of meat were found accompanying both men and women into the next world. In spite of this disaster, however, the site still exercised a hold on the imagination of the local people and in the fourth century A.D., a small stone-built temple of Romano-Celtic type was erected here.

Finds from the Maiden, including the *ballista*, can now be seen, excellently displayed, in the Dorset County Museum, Dorchester. *See* **Dorchester, Native Background, Temples and Religion.**

Left and above, the latest techniques are being employed in the new excavations at the east gate of the hillfort.

MALTON

The visible remains at Malton are now confined to earthworks but, because half of the fort area is now open ground, you can get a good impression here of the size of an auxiliary base, although at 8·4 acres it is an unusually large one. The defences include a double ditch on three sides and a single one on the south-east. The original earthen rampart had a stone wall added to it in the reign of Trajan at roughly the same time as the fortress at York was rebuilt in stone. The army had obviously decided they were here to stay.

A civilian settlement, or *vicus*, grew up on the south-east side of the fort towards the river and it had a defensive rampart on its north-east side which can still be made out. Across the river, in what is now Norton, there was an industrial suburb where pottery and metalworking took place. A remarkable find from here is the inscription indicating the presence of a goldsmith's shop of which a cast can be seen in Malton Museum. The *Pax Romana* in the Vale of Pickering had obviously brought the prosperity required for a steady market in fine jewellery.

Other finds in the museum include part of an inscription referring to the Ala Picentiana, a cavalry regiment from Gaul who garrisoned the fort in the later second century A.D. *See* **York.**

MALTON
(Derventio)
North Yorkshire
OS 100 SE 790720
Malton is 18 miles north-east of York, from which it is reached by the A64. The fort is on the right-hand side of the Pickering Road, a short way from the town centre.

When we think of the Romans in Britain, we do not immediately think of Manchester – Bath, Colchester and York maybe, but not Manchester. Yet here – at the junction between two important Roman roads, one running from York to Chester, and the other running north to Ribchester and ultimately to Carlisle – a fort, Mamucium (Manchester), was established under Agricola in about A.D. 79. This was, of course, constructed in turf and timber, but in the early third century A.D., it was rebuilt in stone and the north gate and part of the wall has recently been reconstructed in full. In the heart of one of Britain's leading industrial cities, therefore, we have a most instructive and valuable resource for the study of Roman military architecture for which no amount of learned words can be a substitute. *See* **The Army.**

MANCHESTER
(Mamucium)
Greater Manchester
OS 109 SJ 835975
Manchester is 197 miles from London. Use th M6 or the good train service from Euston Station, London. The fort is just off Deansgate.

NORTH LEIGH

Oxfordshire
OS 164 SP 397155
To reach the villa, take the A34
from Oxford, turn left before
Woodstock onto the A4095, and
then take the first right after Long
Hanborough. After about 1 mile,
there is a track leading to the site.

At North Leigh, we are in the classic villa country around the Thames tributaries in the valleys of the eastern Cotswolds; indeed, the character of the area has not changed greatly since Roman times and great country houses of the eighteenth and nineteenth centuries still abound here. Then, as now, the source of wealth was agriculture and, for the Roman Britons, there was a happy combination of fertile land and good communications, in this case, along Akeman Street which runs from the small town of Alchester, near Bicester (Oxfordshire), to Cirencester. It is frustrating, however, that we know very little of the day-to-day workings of the villa economy, since few of their farm buildings have been

examined. The efforts of antiquaries and archaeologists have largely gone into looking at the main houses, with special emphasis on the search for mosaic pavements or bath houses. North Leigh is no exception to this, although extensive outbuildings have been detected to the south-west of the villa by aerial photography which can pick up wall lines not visible on the ground.

The buildings you will see today are two wings of an establishment which surrounded three sides of a courtyard, the fourth being closed off with a wall. Notice how a corridor ran around the yard in front of the rooms which would have allowed a measure of privacy for the residents not possible in a dwelling where everyone lived in a single room or in a few interconnecting rooms. North Leigh is still something of a contrast, however, to the prototype courtyard villa at Fishbourne, where absolute privacy within the great garden court was possible, since the main entrance to the villa was through the courtyard where, no doubt, much of the work of the house and estate was also carried on.

While visiting the site be sure to see the fine mosaic with a geometric pattern, executed by the Corinium School, in the main living room which was also heated by an underfloor hypocaust.
See **Fishbourne, Villas.**

Access to this interesting site is via the private track to Lower Riding Farmhouse.

PEVENSEY

(Anderida)
East Sussex
OS 199 TQ 644048
Pevensey is 6 miles north-east of
Eastbourne on the A259. The castle
lies near the village centre.

The *Notitia Dignitatum*, which lists military dispositions of the late fourth century A.D., is the contemporary document referring to the *Litus Saxonicum*, or "Saxon Shore" defences, and its commanding officer, the *comes* or count, but presumably the system had been developing over some time and Pevensey seems to be a late addition. Although, in this sense, it is the odd man out, it remains, thanks to the reuse of the walls by the medieval castle, one of the best preserved "Saxon Shore" forts and one of the most instructive for visitors.

We do not know the exact year of construction, but it probably dates to the late 330s or 340s – a time when the political situation began to deteriorate again following the death of the Emperor Constantine in A.D. 337. He was succeeded by his three sons, of whom Constantine II initially held the west until he was defeated and killed in battle with his brother, Constans. This was only a prelude, however, to further internecine strife which seriously weakened the armies and defences of the empire.

It was probably during Constans's reign that Pevensey was built and he is known to

have visited Britian in A.D. 343, perhaps to restore old defences and construct new ones. The strategic position of the fort is no longer apparent, as the sea has receded since Roman times, but originally it commanded a marshy estuary. The walls have an unusual oval plan, a long way from the regular playing-card shape of the early forts, and there are bastions for artillery. As you inspect the walls, notice the changes in the style of construction which occur at intervals: there are, for example, variations in the frequency of tile courses and in the usage of bands of green sandstone. It has been suggested that this is due to changes in building gangs, although why each gang should wish to distinguish its work in this way is unclear. The garrison recorded at Pevensey in the *Notitia Dignitatum* is the numerus Abulcorum, part of the field army rather than frontier troops. We should remember that the man in charge of the Saxon Shore, specifically referred to as a frontier, or *limes*, is named a *comes* – a title normally used for a field commander rather than a commander of frontier troops.
See **Burgh Castle, The Army, Emperors in Britain.**

Top, the great west gate of Anderida, and above, some other aspects of this important and spectacular ancient monument.

PIERCEBRIDGE

(Morbium)

County Durham

OS 93 NZ 211156

The village is some 7 miles north of Scotch Corner on the B6275. The fort remains are by the church in the village centre. The bridge abutment is reached by a path on the right-hand side of the road, just before you enter the village and just after a bridge and sharp left-turn in the road.

Piercebridge lies on Dere Street, the main Roman road to the north at the point where it meets the River Tees. There was probably a fort here built by Agricola, but little evidence for it has been found. You can, however, see the remains of a bridge which carried the road over the river as the course of the Tees has moved away northwards since Roman times.

The remains of a number of piers survive, but at the south end of the site you will see the well-preserved southern abutment, or pier, which stood against the river bank. Around its base are flat stones laid to prevent the river scouring a deeper channel and so undermining the bridge. No trace, of course, remains of the timber superstructure.

A new fort was built at Piercebridge in about A.D. 270, which interestingly retains the old style of fortification used in the early Roman period rather than adopting new ideas in military architecture which can be seen in the "Saxon Shore" forts, for example. It still has the playing-card shape with rounded corners and there are no projecting bastions. An area on the east side of the fort has recently been laid out for display and you can see the remains of the east gate, which has two carriageways with a guard chamber on each side, and the fort wall. There is a double-ditch system beyond and on the berm, as the space between the wall and inner ditches is called, there are some irregular pits thought to be *lilia*, or lilies, as they were ironically called. Like those at Rough Castle on the Antonine Wall, they originally had camouflaged pointed stakes in the bottom intended to discomfort an attacker.

See **The Army.**

The bridge abutment at Piercebridge.

Few other sites in the western part of the empire give the traveller a better impression of military architecture in the later Roman period than Portchester Castle. The fort, which commands a fine view of what are now the approaches to Portsmouth harbour, originally formed part of the scheme of defensive works protecting the coast against seaborne barbarian invaders. Known as the "Saxon Shore", its exact date of construction is uncertain, but it may belong to the reign of the usurper, Carausius, "that pirate" as he was known at the court of the legitimate Emperor Maximian. Carausius was, however, reasonably successful at getting rid of pirates from Germanic areas outside the empire, and it was this that eventually gave him ideas above his station. Since Portchester must have been associated with Carausius's forces, it is of some interest that excavations have shown the first period of occupation to have ended in A.D. 296, about the time of the defeat of Carausius's successor, Allectus, by Constantius Chlorus. The fort was not reoc- cupied until around A.D. 340 when barbarian raids were again becoming a problem.

The defensive wall forms a near perfect square and survives more or less intact, except where it is interrupted by the Norman Castle in the south-west corner. It is over 20 feet high and fourteen of the original external bastions still survive. Although the walling has been much patched in medieval and later times, the Roman work, which is flint with tile bonding courses, can be seen in many places. Unlike an early Roman fort, it has no internal ramparts and so is much more like a medieval castle.

Extra defence was provided by ditches, double on the landward side and single on the others, with the sea probably protecting the east side. The Roman gates have disap- peared but they were evidently formed by inturning the wall to form small forecourts in front of the entrances in which an enemy might be trapped and fired on.
See **Burgh Castle, Richborough, The Army.**

PORTCHESTER

(Portus Adurni)
Hampshire
OS 196 SU 625045
The castle is signposted in Portchester on the A27 between Fareham and Portsmouth.

The remains of the fort bath house, or Walls Castle as it is known locally, are all that survive today of the fort at Ravenglass. They enjoy a pleasant wooded setting, however, and are well worth a visit since the walls, in places, stand to a height of about 12 feet – sufficient height to preserve a number of arched doorways and windows which are fea- tures not usually seen in Britain's Roman buildings today. Notice also the round- headed niche in one wall, which must orig- inally have held a votive statue, and the unusually well-preserved stretch of rendering made pink by the inclusion of small fragments of broken brick and tile.

The fort itself lay to the west of the baths near the sea, which doubtless suited the gar- rison named in the *Notitia Dignitatum* as the First Cohort of Morinians recruited from the Calais–Boulogne area on the French coast. Little is known of the fort's history, but it would have formed a southern adjunct to the Cumberland Coast defensive system which ran south from the last fort on Hadrian's Wall at Bowness-on-Solway.
See **Carlisle, Hardknott, Bath Houses.**

RAVENGLASS

(Glannoventa)
Cumbria
OS 96 SD 087961
Ravenglass is 18 miles south of Whitehaven, just off the A595. After leaving the main road, look for a path on the left which is signposted to the bath house.

The fort at Ribchester occupied an important strategic position where the military road which runs north from Manchester to Burrow in Lonsdale and Carlisle crosses the River Ribble whose valley formed an important east-west route through the Pennines to the sea. Its location may, therefore, be closely compared with the nearby fort at Lancaster, also on a road-river junction. Both sites reflect the splendid eye for the lie of the land pos- sessed by the governor Agricola.

The Agricolan defences consisted, as was usual for the period, of a ditch and a clay and turf rampart. At Ribchester the rampart rested on a base of horizontal logs to give it extra stability. This is known as a "corduroy" and is a common Roman military device. Under Trajan, a stone wall was put in front of the rampart. Although one-third of the fort has been removed by river erosion, the defences can still be made out in a field west of the church. All that is otherwise visible is in the grounds of the museum, where the east end of two granaries, have been exposed.

The garrison in the Trajanic fort was evidently the Second Ala of Asturian cavalry from Spain who were transferred in the third century A.D. to Chesters. The famous bronze parade helmet, now in the British Museum, was probably the property of one of their troopers. By the late second century A.D., the Asturians had been replaced by a regiment of Sarmatian cavalry. They were part of a force of 8,000 compulsorily recruited by the Emperor Marcus Aurelius during campaigns across the Danube in what is now Hungary. The use of men from outside the empire at this time was unusual, although it became common practice in the later Roman period.

We do not know how the men from the Balkans took to their new homeland, but many of them seem to have made their homes in the area following discharge. Evi- dence for this is found in the *Ravenna Cos- mography* – a seventh-century list of places in the empire which is clearly a copy of a Roman text – where Ribchester is referred to as Bremetennacum Veteranorum, implying a settlement of veterans.
See **The Army.**

RIBCHESTER

(Bremetennacum)
Lancashire
OS 102 SD 650350
Ribchester is about 5 miles north- west of Blackburn. Turn left off the A666 at Whilpshire onto the B6245. In the village, turn down to the river, and then right where you will find the museum next to the churchyard. Ribchester is a most attractive stone-built village and surprisingly unspoilt, considering it is so near to industrial south Lancashire.

Burials
To the Divine Shades

The burial practices of Roman Britain were very diverse and reflected many different religious and social customs, but there is now a good deal of evidence for the subject in the form of funerary monuments and finds from a number of large-scale cemetery excavations. Roman law forbade burial inside settlements, and so cemeteries were usually located immediately outside them, often along main roads. As Britain's towns have expanded into what were sparsely occupied suburbs, the graves have been rediscovered.

In the immediate pre-Roman period, native burial customs included both cremation and inhumation of the body unburnt, but cremation in south-eastern England seems to have been introduced by the Belgic settlers who were arriving at the time of Caesar's invasions in 55 and 54 B.C. Some of their burials were lavishly furnished. The Lexden tumulus in Colchester, for example, contained imported amphorae, wine jars, a bronze boar, a silver medallion of the Emperor Augustus and strands of gold thread, possibly from a garment.

After the Roman conquest, cremation became the usual mode of burial until the third century A.D. The body of the deceased was burnt at a special cremation site, or *ustrina*, and the ashes were then placed in a container, usually a pottery urn but on occasions a lead or glass vessel, for burial in the cemetery. Other objects or grave goods might also be placed in the graves as offerings to the gods of the underworld or to the spirit of the deceased; and could include pots containing food and drink, jewellery or toilet items, such as ointment jars and mirrors. More unusual grave goods, such as lamps, dice, iron tools or hobnail boots are also known. Good examples of cremation grave groups are to be seen in the Castle Museum, Colchester and the Yorkshire Museum, York.

The majority of cremation graves were probably marked by simple earthen mounds, but the practice of erecting carved funerary monuments also began in the early Roman period and was especially favoured by members of the army and provincial administration. Military tombstones have been found in all the major centres and convey a wealth of information about the uniforms, equipment, ranks and origins of the soldiers. A well-known tombstone from Chester, for example, shows Caecilius Avitus who was an *optio*, the second in command to a centurion, of the Twentieth Legion from a *colonia* now known as Merida, in Spain. He wears a heavy cloak, and in one hand holds a staff and in the other a square writing tablet case. His inscription concludes with the letters, H.F.C., a very common abbreviation for *heres faciendum curavit*, meaning that the stone was erected by his heirs. Tombstones might also be set up by burial clubs to which soldiers would have made regular contributions.

By the early third century A.D., cremation had largely gone out of fashion and inhumation became the preferred mode of burial. The reason for this change is not altogether clear, but it may be related to the spread of new religious beliefs involving ideas of resurrection. Excavations seem to show that inhumation graves were, again, quite often furnished, usually with pots or jewellery, until the middle of the fourth century A.D. when the practice became much less common. Graves also assume an almost universal, east – west alignment at this time. Both these developments may be due to the spread of Christianity.

Inhumations in coffins is fairly common in late Roman graves; they were usually wooden, but lead and stone sarcophagi are also known. A fine collection of the stone variety comes from York, many of which give biographical details. One lady, for example, is referred to as "*honesta femina*", meaning she belonged to the upper ranks of Roman citizens known as "*honestiores*", as opposed to the vast majority who were *humiliores*. She predeceased her husband, Caecilius Rufus, who may well have been a *decurion* to judge by his social rank and died aged only 27 years, 9 months and 4 days. Her burial had been arranged by Caecilius Musicus, her husband's *libeus*, or freed slave.

The majority of the population, of course, could not afford a stone coffin, but we can learn a great deal about them through a study of the bodies themselves. Careful study of skeletons from cemeteries at Cirencester, York and elsewhere show, for example, that the average height of Roman males was about 5 feet, 6 inches and of females, 5 feet, 2 inches. This is closely comparable with the British population up to the Second World War, although advances in nutrition since then mean we are now, on average, rather taller. Age at death can also be estimated; it appears that, at birth, life expectancy was fairly low since infant mortality was extremely high. As many as 40 per cent of babies died at birth or in the first 18 months or so of life. On reaching childhood, however, life expectancy was about 40 years and, as in most ancient populations, men lived, on average, rather longer than women largely because of the hazards of childbirth. It is rarely possible to ascertain the cause of death from a skeleton – the *ballista* bolt in a man's spine from Maiden Castle is a rare find, indeed. Certain diseases do appear in bone, however, so we know that the Romano-Britons did suffer from polio and certain forms of tuberculosis and syphilis, but the most common identifiable pathological condition is osteo-arthritis caused by strain on joints at the shoulder, hip, knee, and so on. The high incidence of this disease suggests a population who engaged in regular heavy manual work – women just as much as men. Anyone free of osteo-arthritis, therefore, is likely to have been in a very privileged social position. The majority of the population, however, whether rich or poor, probably died in epidemics of infectious diseases such as cholera and smallpox against which there was no cure.

See **Colchester, London – British Museum, York.**

RICHBOROUGH
(Rutupiae)
Kent
OS 179 TR 321598
The Roman fort and amphitheatre lie almost 1 mile north of Sandwich on a minor road, signposted off the A257 to Canterbury.

The Roman army, not accustomed to maritime enterprises, regarded crossing the Ocean as a great adventure not to be undertaken lightly and Britain, furthermore, was an island of great mystery lying beyond the world's end. In A.D. 43, therefore, in spite of the knowledge of Julius Caesar's successful voyages, the troops of Aulus Plautius delayed the invasion by a mutiny. This was only quelled, according to Cassius Dio's well-known account, when Narcissus, a freed slave, and yet one of the Emperor Claudius's ministers, came to address the troops and remind them of their duty. The legionaries, all Roman citizens, found the spectacle so ridiculous that they shouted "Io Saturnalia!", recalling the festival when slaves dress in their master's clothes, and the trouble was over. In due course, the bulk of the army, if not all of it, made up of four legions and a corresponding number of auxiliary troops, 40,000 men in all, made landfall on the Kent coast at Richborough (Rutupiae), a site which was to remain at the heart of Romano-British history for much of the following 350 years.

Surprisingly, Julius Caesar had missed Richborough, but although the coast line has changed since Roman times, it was clearly an ideal harbour and Plautius's army had soon set up a major supply base here with a number of large storehouses, two of which are marked out on the site today. Richborough retained this role in army supplies until about A.D. 85–90, when a large monument thought to have been a triumphal arch commemorating the conquest was erected on the site. Only its cruciform base survives today, however.

In the second century A.D., Richborough was eclipsed by Dover as a port, although occupation of an official nature, perhaps in the form of a *mansio*, continued. In the mid-third century A.D., the site began to assume a role in the coastal defences of Britain and the triumphal arch was surrounded by a triple ditch system, prominent again today after excavation. The role of this fortlet may have been to signal the arrival of hostile ships, rather in the way the Scarborough signal station worked in the late fourth century A.D..

At some stage between about A.D. 280 and 290 the arch was demolished, and the triple ditches were filled in prior to the construction of a larger fort with stone walls and projecting towers. The walls still stand over 20 feet high in places, and notice how the pattern of facing stones varies from place to place as at Pevensey, suggesting the work of different construction teams. A double-ditch system runs around the walls, but notice, again, that on the west side there are three ditches for a short distance where it would seem that digging had begun on the wrong line – an unusual mistake for the Roman army.

Richborough was now part of the "Saxon Shore" defences and the initiative for its construction was probably that of the Emperor Probus (A.D. 276–82), but it soon fell into the hands of the usurper Carausius, who ruled Britain and parts of northern France until A.D. 294. Carausius, no doubt, used Richborough along with the other "Saxon" forts to resist the legitimate emperor in the west, Maximian, who found it difficult to challenge his command of the seas. Taking advantage of this situation, Carausius issued coins associating himself with his "brothers", Maximian and the co-emperor in the east, Diocletian. In A.D. 293, however, Constantius Chlorus, later Emperor Constantius I, a man of stern resolve, arrived to take charge of the situation and managed to take Boulogne from Carausius, whereupon dissension broke out in the usurper's camp, and he was murdered by his minister, Allectus, whose reign was soon brought to an end.

After Britain had been reunited with the

rest of the empire, Richborough remained a key point in the defences of Britain and according to the *Notitia Dignitatum*, became the base for the Second Legion, originally based at Caerleon. Occupation evidently continued into the early fifth century A.D. and a small church of this period, along with a timber baptistery containing a tile-built font have recently been identified here. Coins of the latest Roman issues are also much more common than at other comparable sites.
See **Burgh Castle, Pevensey, Emperors in Britain.**

Left, a modern cover for the ancient, post-Roman, octagonal font discovered here. Below, the enduring strength of mortared rubble walls is very evident at Richborough.

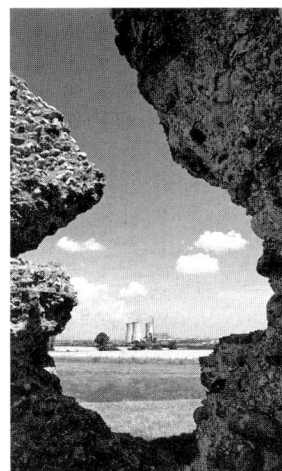

By the early fourth century A.D., the villa at Rockbourne must have presented a pleasing prospect of modest but civilized rural life, with a central courtyard, probably including a garden or orchard, surrounded on three sides not only by well-appointed domestic buildings but also by agricultural buildings and workshops. Like most British villas, this was a working farm.

The history of the site had begun in the late Iron Age with a native hut. In the late first century A.D., a modest rectangular house with stone, used at least in the wall footings, was erected. In the second century A.D., this was replaced by a new and larger house which eventually became the west wing of the villa which, along with the north wing, included the main living rooms. At the corner of this L-shaped complex, there was a bath house and in the remains of the *caldarium*, or warm room, notice that the hypocaust is constructed, unusually, on pairs of roof ridge tiles set

ROCKBOURNE
Hampshire
OS 184 SU 120170
The villa is about a $\frac{1}{2}$ mile south of Rockbourne Village, which is itself 4 miles north-west of Fordingbridge.

117

on end. There are also box tiles set in the walls which would have improved the circulation of hot air. In the room heated by a hypocaust next to the baths, a milestone of the Emperor Tetricus was found. He reigned from A.D. 271–3, and was the last of the so-called "Gallic emperors" who ruled much of the western Roman Empire independently from Rome between A.D. 260 and 274. This milestone is in the museum, along with another referring to the Emperor Decius (A.D. 249–51), whose brief reign is principally known for the persecution of Christians.

As you go east along the north wing, notice a fine geometric mosaic on which, if you look carefully, there are burnt patches – the result of braziers which were used for heating in the absence of a hypocaust. Towards the east end of the wing there is another bath suite with two further mosaics. Unlike Chedworth,

where the two bath suites offered either steam or dry heat, both Rockbourne baths were of the steam type. The reason for having two may be a simple modesty which required the segregation of men and women.

Beyond the northern baths and in the south wing, there were smithies where agricultural tools could be manufactured and repaired, and there are a number of these in the museum. Although villas relied on towns for some manufactured goods, they were self-sufficient in many areas and probably became more so as communications deteriorated in the later fourth century A.D.

At some time after A.D. 400, the buildings here fell into disrepair and it is suggested that a skeleton found in one of the rooms is of a man who died when the roof fell in on him. *See* **North Leigh.**

ST ALBANS
(Verulamium)
Hertfordshire
OS 166 TL 134074
St Albans is 23 miles north of London on Watling Street, the A5183. The modern city owes its origins to the medieval abbey, and travellers will enjoy a stroll in the abbey precinct and neighbouring streets.

When you stand in the Roman theatre at St Albans and look north-east, across Roman Watling Street to the medieval Abbey Church on the hill, you are looking at one of the most important sites in Britain for both its urban and religious history. On that hill, Alban, a high-ranking citizen of the Roman town, was martyred, probably in A.D. 209 in the presence of Geta, son of Emperor Septimius Severus who was campaigning in Britain at the time. At this spot, a shrine grew up which is referred to by the Anglo-Saxon monk, the Venerable Bede, in the eighth century A.D. Subsequently, the medieval abbey was founded here and you will note that its Norman tower is constructed almost entirely of Roman brick and tile. Outside the Abbey precinct, the medieval town flourished and lies at the heart of modern St Albans.

The Roman town, whose Latin name prob-

ably means "above the marshes" lies by the banks of the river Ver, the successor to a nearby pre-Roman settlement of the Catuvellauni people. This was one of Britain's first towns since, according to Tacitus, it was a *municipium* by A.D. 60 when it was one of the places destroyed by Boudicca.

Recovery from the disaster was slow, but by A.D. 79 a forum had been built, now under the site of St Michael's Church, and part of a dedicatory inscription bearing the name of the governor Agricola, who is known to have encouraged the erection of public buildings, may be seen in the museum. Another disaster struck in the mid-second century A.D. when a fire, a constant hazard in ancient towns, swept through the main streets. On this occasion rebuilding was rapid and one new structure of this period was the theatre which has been fully excavated and is on public display.

The original building did not have the classic semi-circular form, instead the stage occupied one side of an almost circular arena suggesting that the focus of activities was in the *orchestra*, which strictly speaking means dance floor, in front of it. The structure you will see today has a rather larger stone-built *proscaenium*, or stage, with a Corinthian column providing an impression of the original backdrop to it, which was formed by a complete row of such columns. You can also see a massive buttressed outer wall erected in the fourth century A.D. to retain the banks of seating. To the south-west of the theatre was a temple; this close spatial relationship is repeated at Canterbury and Colchester and suggests that the theatre was extensively used for religious ceremonies.

Because the focus of settlement at St Albans has moved away from the valley, Verulamium has remained largely open ground since Roman times and large-scale excavations have been possible here. A large number of ordinary town buildings have been examined, for example, which are usually described as "strip houses".

One of the most exciting results of the excavations was to show that town life probably flourished here well into the troubled times of the later fourth century A.D. and a number of new mosaics were laid in its last decades. As at Wroxeter, moreover, there was occupation here in the fifth century A.D. up to the time of the recorded visit of St Germanus in A.D. 429 and probably well beyond, which suggests that the inhabitants were able to reach some form of accommodation with the Anglo-Saxons who were flooding into the south-east of England at this time.

See **Wroxeter, Towns, Public Buildings.**

The orchestra and stage of Verulamimium's theatre.

In A.D. 367, all the barbarian people who were harassing the coasts of Britain managed somehow to unite in what is known as the *Barbarica Conspiratio*, or Barbarian Conspiracy. One group of conspirators were the Picts from what is now Scotland, who evaded the Hadrian's Wall frontier by the simple expedient of sailing around it. To prevent this recurring, a series of signal stations were erected on the Yorkshire coast which could alert the army at Malton or York to any impending danger. The only one where any significant remains survive is in the confines of Scarborough Castle.

Erosion of the cliff face has removed some of the site, but there was clearly an outer ditch with an entrance causeway on the landward side, an outer wall with rounded bastions at the corners, and in the centre a rectangular timber tower which may have been as high as 100 feet, comparable that is to the Norman Castle Keep close by.

The signal stations remained in use until at least A.D. 394 after which their occupation apparently came to a violent end. At Goldsborough, the next signal station but one northwards, for example, excavations discovered the skeletons of a man, face down, apparently stabbed in the back, and of another man lying near him under whom was a large dog, his paws around the man's shoulders. Was the last act of the faithful hound to take on his master's assailant? We shall never know, but travellers might care to reflect that these signal stations are only the first in a long line of coastal defences on this stretch of coast. On your way to Wheeldale Roman road, you are sure to see the great "golf balls" of Fylingdales radar station which is the latest of these.

SCARBOROUGH
North Yorkshire
OS 101 TA 052892
Scarborough is 41 miles north east of York and is reached via the A64. The castle is on high ground, a little to the north-east of the town centre. Scarborough is one of Britain's most elegant seaside resorts and well worth a visit.

The defensive walls of Calleva Atrebatum, once home to some 4000 inhabitants.

Travellers who have visited North Africa and seen Roman towns such as Lepcis Magna or Dougga, where acres of streets and buildings still survive in remarkable condition will, at first sight, inevitably be disappointed by the towns of Britain which have long since been dismantled. At Silchester (Calleva Atrebatum), however, it is possible, at least in the mind's eye, to picture a Romano-British town as it was in its heyday. For not only is it one of a small group which have hardly been built on since Roman times, but extensive excavations on the 100-acre site in the last century have provided a remarkably complete plan of the streets and buildings. In typical Roman fashion the streets, almost invariably metalled, formed a regular grid; the public buildings lay in the centre and there was an area restored for temples. Shops occupied many of the street frontages and houses of a wide variety of plan forms were found in almost every *insula*. By counting them, a maximum population estimate of about 4,000 has been arrived at. Around the perimeter ran the defences and much of the wall erected in the second century A.D.

Unfortunately, we know little of the sequence of events in Silchester since, at the time of the excavations, there was little understanding of the need to relate datable finds, such as coins or pottery, to buildings. The techniques used were, moreover, only able to locate masonry structures, although recent work has demonstrated the presence of timber buildings which on the forum site, for example, predate those in stone.

In outline, however, we know that there was a native settlement of the Atrebates here in the pre-Roman period which acquired defences shortly after the conquest in A.D. 43, when it may have been part of Cogidubnus's kingdom. In the mid-70s, possibly after Cogidubnus's death, a major planning effort which involved the erection of the forum and perhaps the amphitheatre took place. This must have been part of the kind of official encouragement to urbanization that we hear of Agricola embarking on in Tacitus's biography. Evidently, it was a success as growth was steady.

Romanization also manifests itself in some of Silchester's more minor discoveries such as, for example, a graffito scratched on a tile which echoes the opening of the second book of Virgil's *Aeneid*. Evidence of another sort was provided by barrel staves of silver fir which does not normally grow north of the Mediterranean region, suggesting the import of fine wines from the Bordeaux area of Gaul.

In the later Roman period, Silchester appears to have been another of Britain's towns with a Christian community, for an apsed basilican building found in the forum *insula* has been interpreted as a church. Although there is no incontrovertible proof of this, especially as its focal point was at the west not the east end, its location analogous to that of the Lincoln church does imply offi-

SILCHESTER
(Calleva Atrebatum)
Hampshire
OS 175 SU 639625
Silchester is some 9 miles north of Basingstoke and 11 miles south of Reading. Follow the minor road from the north east corner of Silchester Common for about 1½ miles to the parish church of St Mary the Virgin. Park here to explore the fine church as well as the Roman town's walls.

cial approval at a time when Christianity was the empire's state religion.

The urban settlement which emerged in this area in medieval times was at Reading rather than Silchester but, thanks to this, the *genius loci,* (spirit of place) of the Roman town is still very much alive and in the summer months excavations sponsored by Hampshire County Council, the site owners, show it still has many secrets to reveal.
See **Chichester, Lincoln, Towns, Public Buildings.**

STANWICK

North Yorkshire
OS 92 NZ 185120
Stanwick is some 9 miles north of Richmond. To reach the site, either take the B6274 from Richmond, or the A66 from Scotch Corner and then the B6274 which brings you to Forcett Church. Turn right here and, after about two-thirds of a mile, turn right again for Stanwick St John Church.

The great circuit of earthworks at Stanwick, which enclose some 600 acres of rolling north Yorkshire countryside, betray little trace of the dramatic events to which they once bore witness. These events can be traced both in the works of the Roman author, Tacitus, and in the excavation report of Sir Mortimer Wheeler.

In the early years of the conquest, the Romans were content to contain the far-flung tribes of Brigantia within their mountainous homeland, but in A.D. 51, Caratacus, who had led the Welsh tribes in their resistance, fled north to the court of Queen Cartimandua. His hopes of safety were, however, misplaced and he was handed over to the Romans in chains. At this, a quarrel seems to have broken out between Cartimandua and her consort, Venutius – "pre-eminent in military skill", as Tacitus calls him, and it may be on this occasion that he based himself within the earliest enclosure at Stanwick of some 17 acres in an area around where Stanwick church now stands, called "The Tofts". At first, Cartimandua's forces were successful and captured Venutius's brother and relatives. "But", Tacitus goes on, "her enemies infuriated and goaded by fears of humiliating feminine rule, invaded her kingdom with a powerful force of picked warriors". In the event, a Roman force had to be sent to save her. Following this, Wheeler suggests that a new enclosure of 130 acres defended by a ditch and rampart, revetted with a stone wall, was built at Stanwick.

In A.D. 69, when Rome was preoccupied with the problems of the imperial succession, Venutius appears to have rebelled again against Cartimandua who was losing popularity as a result of an affair with his squire, Vellocatus, and had to be removed to safety by the Romans who now saw the need to crush Venutius once and for all. It is, perhaps, in preparation for this final battle that Venutius enlarged his fortified area yet again so as to accommodate, at least on a temporary basis, his followers, their families and, just as vital, their livestock. The alarm created by the approach of the Ninth Legion as the Brigantes worked on their defences seems to be documented at the south gate which Wheeler found had been left unfinished and then hurriedly blocked before abandonment.

The course of the Stanwick earthworks can easily be traced with a large-scale map and there is a restored section through the second period defences on the north-west side of the circuit.
See **Native Background.**

WALL

(Letocetum)
Staffordshire
OS 139 SK 098067
The village of Wall is about 2 miles south of Lichfield on a minor road. It is also 14 miles north of Birmingham. Take the A5127 to the village of Shenstone, turn left at the next roundabout onto the A5 (Roman Watling Street), and you will see a sign off to Wall on the right.

The earliest Roman presence at Wall was probably a fort established during the advance outwards from the Fosse Way frontier in the 50s. Military occupation was, however, brief and eventually Wall became a village and staging point on Watling Street between London and Wroxeter. This may explain the presence of a second-century A.D. building whose footings can still be seen, which is known as the *mansio,* or inn. It has a group of small rooms thought to be for the accommodation of travellers, ranged around a courtyard.

To the south-west of the *mansio* is the bath house. It has a complex history, beginning in the first century A.D., after which it was gradually expanded and altered to reach its present form in the fourth century A.D. All the different rooms, each with its own function, can be identified, although the hypocaust *pilae* in the *caldarium* have had to be reburied for protection against the weather. There is a useful reconstruction drawing in the adjacent site museum.

The total extent of Roman settlement at Wall may, at one time, have been about 30 acres, but little else is known about it.
See **Roads.**

WHEELDALE

North Yorkshire
OS 100 SE 807980
The site can be found by taking the A169 north from Pickering. After 13 miles, turn left to the village of Goathland. From here signs direct you along a minor road to within a short distance of the Roman road.

The Roman road on Wheeldale Moor, known locally as Wade's Causeway after a legendary giant, is a remarkable survival. The course of other roads can be detected from the appearance of their *agger* as a low linear mound, but here it is possible to see the larger stones, which made up the base layer of metalling. Notice also a few original drainage culverts with their cover stones still in place.

The exposed section was originally part of a road running north-east–south-west which connected a fort at Lease Rigg near Whitby with the fort at Malton passing close to Cawthorn camps on the way.
See **Roads.**

Lead was a metal of great importance in Roman Britain and was energetically mined under state supervision. Since lead does not, like iron, corrode significantly when in contact with water, it was extensively used in plumbing. Lead pipes stamped with the name of the governor Agricola have, for example, been found at Chester and large leadsheets lined the Great Bath at Bath. In the later Roman period, new uses for lead included the manufacture of coffins.

The most productive lead mines in Britain were probably in the Mendips in Somerset where a number of stamped lead ingots or "pigs" have been found, but the metal was also produced in Northumberland and this probably explains the role of the fort at Whitley Castle. It is sited on the road known as the Maiden Way, which runs up to Hadrian's Wall at Carvoran Fort, and guards the valley of the south Tyne. As at Dolaucothi, the soldiers would have supervised both the extraction process and the subsequent distribution of the metal.

A great feature of the fort is the defensive ditches, up to eight or nine on the west side, which lacks any natural advantage, and their state of preservation can only be paralleled at Ardoch. As you enter the fort from the nearby farm, you pass through the *porta principalis sinistra*; the bath house was just outside the gate and was no doubt supplied with water by the burn in the little valley beyond. Within the fort there are signs of buildings below the grass, but little excavation has been undertaken here to determine their nature.

See **Hadrian's Wall – Wall Town Crag.**

WHITLEY CASTLE
Northumberland
OS 86 NY 695487
Whitley Castle lies a little to the south-west of the A689 some 2 miles north-west of Alston (Cumbria). Park by the telephone box opposite Castle Nook Farm. After asking permission at the farm, follow the path through the farmyard to the fort.

The Roman site at Wroxeter lies below a prominent local landmark known as the Wrekin, and one reason for the establishment of a fortress of the Fourteenth Legion here, in about A.D. 58, may have been the need to keep watch on a hillfort of the local Cornovii tribe on its summit during preparations for the advance into Wales. Subsequently, the fortress was garrisoned by the Twentieth Legion, but it was abandoned by the legion in favour of Chester in about A.D. 87, although a military presence remained here for a little while longer.

There is little evidence for the growth of a civilian settlement here until Hadrian's reign, although an unfinished bath house of the late first century A.D. was found under the later forum. This building, originally a magnificent structure of considerable pretension, lay on the west side of the modern B4380, but all that can be seen here today is a row of column bases which originally supported a colonnade. The site has, however, also produced part of a commemorative inscription, dated A.D. 129–30 from the form used for the Emperor Hadrian's titles, which records the construction of the forum by the *civitas Cornoviorum*; it is now to be seen in Shrewsbury Museum.

Because Wroxeter is now almost deserted, it has been possible to undertake excavations here on a rather larger scale than is usual in a Roman town. In recent years, one part of the programme has been concentrated in the *insula* on the east side of the B4380, where the so-called "Old Work" now stands. This unusually massive piece of surviving masonry formed part of the south wall of the *palaestra*, or exercise hall, of the Hadrianic bath house and to the south of it the remains of the rest of the baths are displayed. The opening in the wall, once a grand doorway, led into the *frigidarium* and beyond this lay the *tepidarium* and *caldarium*; their floors were originally heated with a hypocaust as is shown by an impressive array of replica *pilae* tiles. The furnace, or *praefurnium*, lay at the south end of the building. Notice also the *piscina*, or outdoor swimming pool, which is an unusual addition to a bath complex in chilly Britain.

The *palaestra* itself was originally a massive aisled structure comparable to a medieval cathedral. Excavations have revealed that it fell out of use in A.D. 300 and was carefully dismantled in stages while flimsy timber buildings were erected within it.

During this period the site finds suggest two unusual cults were practised in the area. A pair of eyes in sheet gold and over thirty-five eyes cut out out of wall plaster fragments suggested that a deity with special powers over eye diseases had a temple nearby. Secondly, and more gruesome, a number of human skull pieces were found which seem to have been specially treated with vegetable oil. A few of them indicate scalping and it has been proposed that they were displayed as cult relics.

See **St Albans, Towns, Public Buildings.**

WROXETER
(Viroconium)
Shropshire
OS 126 SJ 566088
Wroxeter is a few miles south-east of Shrewsbury. Take the A5 and then turn right onto the B4380 just after Atcham.

Julia Fortunata and her husband Vercundius Diogenes were leading citizens of one of the most prosperous and cosmopolitan cities of the Roman west. From the inscriptions on her coffin, now in the Yorkshire Museum, we know that she was originally from Sardinia, and from that on his coffin we know not only that he came from Bourges in Gaul, but that he was a *sevir Augustalis*, i.e. a member of the group of six priests who ministered to the cult of the divine emperor in a *colonia*, a town of the highest rank.

Colonial status was probably granted to York in recognition of its rapid growth in the later second century A.D. to a pre-eminent economic and commercial position in the

YORK
(Eburacum)
North Yorkshire
OS 105 SE 600520
York is 209 miles north of London using the M1, A1 and A64.

north of Britain. It was also made capital of Britannia Inferior, lower Britain, one of the two provinces into which the country was divided early in the third century A.D., probably during the reign of the Emperor Caracalla whose father, Septimius Severus had been the first of two emperors to die in York.

One reason for the growth of Roman York is its geographical location: it has easy access to the rest of Britain by road and water, and lies in the heart of rich agricultural land for which it could provide a ready market. The site was originally chosen by the governor Petillius Cerialis who marched north with the Ninth Legion in the early 70s to put an end to the reign of Venutius, the anti-Roman king of the local Brigantes tribe. He made his base for conquest on a low plateau overlooking the north-east bank of the River Ouse which has been the heart of human settlement in York ever since.

Agricola probably refurbished Cerialis's fortress defences, but in the reign of Trajan they were rebuilt in stone – work commemorated by an inscription which originally adorned the fortress's south-east gate and is now in the Yorkshire Museum. it is of particular interest because it carries the last reference to the Ninth Legion in Britain. It was once thought that the Ninth was destroyed in Scotland, but it now seems to have been transferred to the east in about A.D. 120 to be replaced by the Sixth Victrix, or victorious, Legion whose badge was a bull, later used also as the badge of Britannia Inferior.

The defences were rebuilt again in the reign of Septimius Severus, who held court in York while campaigning in the north. A fine piece of the Severan Wall surviving to parapet height can be found at the east corner of the fortress, along with the base of the corner tower. After visiting this site visitors should return to medieval Monk Bar and walk around the city walls for they follow the same line as the north-east and north-west fortress defences. When you arrive at Bootham Bar, you are on the site of the *porta principalis dextra*, or north-west gate.

The Emperor Constantius I also died in York in A.D. 306 and his son, Constantine, of whom there is a twice life-sized bust in the Yorkshire Museum, was acclaimed emperor by the troops here. Constantine was probably the instigator of one of the great glories of military architecture in Britain, the so-called Multangular Tower now to be found in the Museum Gardens. This tower is at the south-west corner of the fortress and was part of a scheme of reconstruction of the whole south-west front which included another tower, similar to the Multangular Tower, at the south-east corner and polygonally fronted interval towers between them. The base of one, in a poor state of repair, can also be seen in Museum Gardens along with a very fine piece of the curtain wall which still stands to almost full height with its small limestone block-facing and tile-bonding courses intact.

A little to the north-east of the Multangular Tower, there is another stretch of Constantinian Wall and the base of an interval tower. Beyond this is the so-called "Anglian Tower", thought to be a seventh-century A.D. attempt to block a gap in the fortress defences. It may, however, be very late Roman since aspects of its construction cannot be paralleled in any other structure of post-Roman date.

Apart from its defences, relatively little is known of the York fortress layout because it is buried deep below the modern city. Some of the walls of the *principia* were, however, found during strengthening work on the Minster foundations and can be seen in the undercroft there. Look out, in particular, for the massive bases of columns, still in place, which held up the roof of the aisled cross-hall. A complete column has been re-erected opposite the south door of the Minster.

In St Sampson's Square, travellers may refresh themselves at the "Roman Bath" public house in which some remains of the legionary bath house excavated in the 1930s can be seen. Connected with the baths was a unique vaulted stone-built sewer, in places 5 feet high. A stretch about 100 feet long was found at the junction of nearby Church Street and Swinegate.

Virtually nothing survives above ground of the civilian settlements in York, although excavations have shown that in the *colonia* on the south-west bank of the river, stone and timber buildings survive in good condition deep below the modern ground level. Some indication of the sophisticated and elegant lifestyle of its inhabitants can, however, be gathered from the displays in the Yorkshire Museum – not only from the funerary monuments, but also from the jewellery, including some very fine pieces in the local jet, glass-ware and metal work. Look out also for the dedication stone from a *Serapeum*, or temple of the god Serapis who was associated with the eastern cult of the Mother Goddess Isis. The inscription suggests that the temple was founded by Claudius Hieronymianus, commander of the Sixth Legion and possibly himself an Egyptian by origin. Another curiosity is a cast of what may be the last inscription from Roman Britain which records the construction, or reconstruction, of one of the Yorkshire coast signal stations at Ravenscar, a little to the north of that at Scarborough.
See **Stanwick, The Army, Towns, Daily Life, Burials.**

GLOSSARY OF CHARACTERS

AGRICOLA Gnaeus Julius Agricola was governor of Britain between A.D. 78 and A.D. 84. Thanks to the biography of his son-in-law, Tacitus, we know a good deal about his life. He was born in the *colonia* of Forum Iulii, now Fréjus in France and served in Britain on two occasions before succeeding Frontinus as governor. During his period of office he campaigned extensively in north Wales, northern England and Scotland where he inflicted a crushing defeat on the Caledonian tribes at Mons Graupius, probably near Aberdeen. His plans for the total conquest of Scotland, based on the fortress at Inchtuthil, were, however, unfulfilled.

ALLECTUS Finance minister to the usurper Carausius and his murderer in A.D. 293. Allectus was defeated and deposed by Constantius Chlorus, in A.D. 296.

AULUS PLAUTIUS The Roman general who led the invasion of Britain in A.D. 43. He then became Britain's first governor. On returning to Rome in A.D. 47, he became the last man to receive an *ovatio*, a form of triumphal celebration.

BOUDICCA (Sometimes known as Boadicea) A true British heroine and, in today's jargon, a freedom fighter. She was the wife of King Prasutagus of the Iceni people in East Anglia until his death in A.D. 60. Following the rough treatment of herself and her family and the forcible seizure of the kingdom by the Romans, she led a revolt against them. After initial success, including the burning of Colchester, London and St Albans, her forces were defeated by the governor Suetonius Paulinus in A.D. 61. Her name literally means "victory", and, according to Tacitus, she was red-headed and "huge of frame, terrifying of aspect and with a harsh voice". Tacitus would be unlikely to approve of her, however, as to the Romans she was, again in today's jargon, a terrorist.

CARATACUS One of the sons of King Cunobelin. Fiercely anti-Roman, he was forced out of his homeland in the south-east of England by the conquest. He fled to become leader of the resistance, first in the territory of the Silures and then among the Ordovices in north Wales. Defeated there in A.D. 51, he sought refuge in the court of Queen Cartimandua of the Brigantes. Unfortunately for him, she turned him over to the Romans. Evidently, his capture made quite a stir in Rome where, according to Tacitus, he made an impressive speech following which he was pardoned.

CARAUSIUS A colourful character who seized power in Britain and parts of northern France in A.D. 286, following successful campaigns as a naval commander against barbarian pirates in the English channel and North Sea. Originally of humble origins in Menapia, now on the coast of Belgium, Carausius appears from his coins, where he is depicted thick necked and hirsute, something of a barbarian himself, albeit one of some pretention judging again by his coins; on one issue there is, for example, an allusion to Virgil's *Aeneid*. After successfully resisting the legitimate emperor in the west, Carausius was murdered by Allectus in A.D. 293, following the loss of Boulogne to Constantius Chlorus.

CARTIMANDUA Queen of the Brigantes, her name literally means "sleek pony", indicating the importance of the horse to Celtic peoples. When she first enters Tacitus's narrative, she is married to Venutius, but after her betrayal of Caratacus, they appear to have fallen out and she was forced to look to Rome for support. Subsequent to this, her popularity waned and she made matters worse by taking Venutius's squire, Vellocatus, as a lover. "Her husband was favoured by the sentiments of all the citizens; the adulterer was supported by the Queen's passion for him and by her savage spirit", as

Tacitus puts it. In A.D. 69 or 70, Venutius rebelled again and Cartimandua had to be removed to safety. Sir Mortimer Wheeler suggested that she was a southerner in origin who had, in some way, inherited the Brigantian kingdom. Since Brigantia's economy was largely pastoral, he put her dissatisfaction with Venutius down to a diet of "unmitigated mutton".

CASSIUS DIO Cassius Dio Cocceianus was a Roman writer who lived in the late second and early third century A.D. He refers to events in Britain from the conquest of A.D. 43 onwards, but his often lively narrative is not always considered entirely reliable except when he is writing about his own times.

CLODIUS ALBINUS Decimus Clodius Albinus was appointed governor of Britain in A.D. 191 or 192 by the Emperor Commodus. Commodus's successor, Septimius Severus made Albinus "Caesar", or junior emperor. In due course, friction between the two men led Albinus to challenge Severus for the throne, but he was defeated at the battle of Lyons in A.D. 197. In the course of his campaign, Albinus must have removed most of the Roman garrison from Britain which may have been the occasion for a spate of defensive works around the province's towns.

COGIDUBNUS Client king of the Atrebatic people in the early years of Roman rule, he styled himself Tiberius Claudius Cogidubnus after the Emperor Claudius. Cogidubnus remained loyal to Rome throughout his life and may have been rewarded with the Fishbourne "proto-palace". Although the larger subsequent palace may have been intended for him, it is likely that he was dead before it was completed.

CUNOBELIN (Or Cunobelinus in Latin) King of the Catuvellauni of south-east England in the first half of the first century A.D.. At his death in about A.D. 40, he was the most powerful native leader in southern Britain. One of his claims to fame is the minting of coins which appeared in considerable numbers during his reign. His burial place is thought to be the Lexden tumulus in Colchester. A romanticized version of his life is the subject of Shakespeare's play, *Cymbeline*.

FRONTINUS Sextus Julius Frontinus was governor of Britain between A.D. 73 or 74 and 77 or 78. His period of office was marked by the establishment of a legionary fortress at Caerleon and campaigns which conquered and pacified the Silures of south Wales, "after a hard struggle, not only against the valour of the enemy, but against the difficulties of the terrain", as Tacitus wrote.

JULIA DOMNA Wife of the Emperor Septimius Severus and a Syrian by origin, Julia Domna was a woman of great character and personality who wielded considerable political authority both in her husband's reign and in that of her son, Caracalla. She was to be greatly saddened, however, by the death of her son Geta at the hands of his brother but – as Cassius Dio, who hated Caracalla, tells us – she was forbidden to show her grief. In statuary Julia Domna is often represented as Ceres and she is known to have taken a great interest in eastern religions.

JUVENAL Famous as the author of *The Sixteen Satires*, Juvenal was born in about A.D. 55 in Spain. He saw military service as the commander of an auxiliary unit in Britain under Agricola. He then spent most of his life in Rome cultivating social contacts. The satires were published in the early second century A.D.

LOLLIUS URBICUS As governor of Britain from A.D. 138 or 139 to perhaps A.D. 144, Quintus Lollius Urbicus was principally concerned with the construction of the Antonine Wall in Scotland.

MARTIAL Marcus Valerius Martial, like Juvenal, was from Spain where he was born in about A.D. 40. He spent much of his time in Rome where he published twelve books of *Epigrams* before returning to die in Spain in about A.D. 104.

PETILLIUS CERIALIS Quintus Petillius Cerialis was governor of Britain from A.D. 71 to A.D. 73 or 74. His first appointment to Britain, however, was as legate of the Ninth Legion at the time of Boudicca's revolt. On one occasion, he barely escaped with his life after being attacked by her forces. His appointment as governor was probably due to friendship with the Emperor Vespasian and his main campaigns were against the Brigantes in the north.

PLATORIUS NEPOS Aulus Platorius Nepos was governor of Britain from A.D. 122 to perhaps A.D. 125. He was appointed by his friend the Emperor Hadrian and his major task was to initiate the construction of Hadrian's Wall.

STILICHO The general, Flavius Stilicho, was a Vandal by birth and, therefore, one of a number of "barbarians" or, at least, men from outside the empire who, in the late fourth century A.D., had risen through the ranks of the army to high office. He married the niece of the Emperor Theodosius and, during the first part of the reign of the Emperor Honorius, who succeeded in A.D. 395, he was the effective ruler in the west. Stilicho was probably the last Roman leader to make a serious attempt to defend Britain, but he was murdered in A.D. 409 as the result of a court intrigue.

SUETONIUS PAULINUS Gaius Suetonius Paulinus was governor of Britain at the time of the Boudiccan revolt. He was evidently taken by surprise by its ferocity and had to make a hurried retreat from north Wales, where he had captured Anglesey, home of the Druids. After defeating Boudicca, Tacitus tells us, he was withdrawn from Britain because, "it was feared that he would abuse their [the Briton's] surrender and punish every offence with undue severity, as if it were a personal injury".

TACITUS Cornelius Tacitus lived from about A.D. 56 to A.D. 120 and is the author of three major sources of information for the early history of Roman Britain: *The Histories*, *The Annals* and *The Agricola*, a biography of his revered father-in-law. He reveals little of himself in his writing, apart from a strong sense of moral rectitude, but he is known to have been of senatorial rank and to have become civilian governor of western Anatolia.

THEODOSIUS Count Theodosius was sent by the Emperor Valentinian I to restore order in Britain after the Barbarian Conspiracy of A.D. 367. His measures probably included rebuilding on Hadrian's Wall, the construction of early-warning signal stations on the Yorkshire coast and the addition of bastions to the walls of towns. Unlike many army commanders of this time, he was a provincial landowner rather than a career soldier.

GLOSSARY OF TERMS

AEDES The shrine in a military headquarters or urban basilica.

AGGER A roman word for the raised embankment on which a road was built.

ALA (plural *alae*) An auxiliary cavalry unit, it could be either 500 or, more rarely, 1,000 strong. The horses had splendid decorative harnesses and the men are often depicted in special parade armour on their tombstones.

APODYTERIUM A changing room in a bath house.

BALLISTA (plural *ballistae*) A large military catapult which fired projectiles of iron or stone. The most famous *ballista* bolt in Britain is that piercing the spine of a man buried at Maiden Castle. *Ballistaria* or *ballista* platforms can still be detected in some forts. In the later Roman period *ballistae* were mounted on bastions projecting from fort walls.

BASILICA A large aisled hall to be found in fort *principiae* or town fora. The basilica was a building type adopted for use by numerous religious cults, including Christianity, who needed space for communal worship.

BONDING-COURSE Layers of tiles or flat stones to be found in a Roman wall which, by running through its complete thickness, help to bind the rubble core to the outer skin of facing stones.

BREASTWORK A breastwork consists of vertical posts and close-set horizontal timbers which serve to retain the front of earthen ramparts. They were not as common in Britain as stacked turf-fronted ramparts.

CALDARIUM The hot steamy room of a bath house.

CAVEA The seating surrounding an amphitheatre arena. In British amphitheatres, the banks underneath the seating were usually of earth or gravel and the seats were often timber, unlike the great amphitheatres of the Mediterranean world which were built throughout in stone.

CENTURION The N.C.O. of the Roman army, a centurion commanded a century of eighty men. Centurions usually rose through the ranks of the legion and were thoroughly experienced and professional soldiers. The senior centurion in a legion commanded the First Cohort and was known as a *primus pilus*.

CHI-RHO The first two letters of Christ's name in Greek. They were used as a monogram on objects and in places used by Christians. Good examples can be seen in the British Museum on vessels in the Water Newton hoard and on the Hinton St Mary mosaic.

CIVITAS (plural *civitates*) A local government administrative area with boundaries usually based on those of pre-Roman communities. They were ruled from a *civitas* capital which, in Britain, were towns deliberately founded for the purpose.

COHORT A unit of the Roman army. A legionary cohort usually consisted of 480 men, although the First Cohort was of double strength. Auxiliary cohorts were units, 500 or 1,000 strong, which were either wholly infantry or consisted of both infantry and some mounted troops.

COLONIA (plural *coloniae*) The highest rank of Roman chartered town. A *colonia*'s inhabitants would be Roman citizens who governed themselves according to a constitution modelled on that of Rome itself. In provinces like Britain, *coloniae* were founded by granting land to legionary veterans. In the later Roman period, the title might be awarded as an honour to some particularly important settlement. York was, for example, made a *colonia*, probably in the early third century A.D. in recognition of its pre-eminent position in the north of England.

COMES Usually translated as count, a *comes* was a title used for a commander of the field army in the fourth century A.D. Theodosius, who was sent to Britain after the Barbarian

Conspiracy of A.D. 367, had the title of count. The commander of the "Saxon Shore" forts is referred to as a *comes* in the *Notitia Dignitatum*, although the officer in charge of frontier troops was more usually known as a *dux*, or duke.

COMITATENSES Soldiers of the *comitatus*, or imperial field army, probably created during the reign of Constantine. They were largely heavily armed cavalry and since they were not tied to a particular province, as the legions had been, they gave the emperor a new flexibility in his military activities.

CONTUBERNIUM (plural *contubernia*) A tent party – a group of eight men who shared a tent while the legion was on campaign, and two rooms when in barracks.

CRENELLATION The regular space at the top of a parapet through which missiles could be fired.

DUX Usually translated as duke, *dux* was a title given to the commander of frontier troops in the late Roman army. The *Dux Britanniarum*, Duke of the Britons, possibly based in York, commanded the frontier troops on Hadrian's Wall in the fourth century A.D.

FRIGIDARIUM The cold room in a bath house where people would take a cold plunge to close the skin's pores after sweating out the dirt.

HYPOCAUST The term refers to the hot air under-floor heating system found in bath houses or the living rooms of well-appointed town houses and villas.

INSULA (plural *insulae*) Literally "island", meaning the space between the streets in the urban grid network.

IRON AGE A term usually used by archaeologists to describe the period between about 700 B.C., when iron technology was first introduced into this country and A.D. 43, the date of the Roman conquest.

LACONICUM A hot room in a bath house which provided dry heat – a Roman version of the sauna.

LATRINE As used in a military context, it means a lavatory or toilet.

LIMITANEI A term used to describe the troops stationed on the frontiers of the empire in the fourth century A.D., as opposed to the higher status, *comitatenses* of the mobile field army.

MANES The spirits of the dead to whom dedications were often made on tombstones, with the formula D.M. standing for *Dis Manibus*.

MANSIO (plural *mansiones*) A guest house used for official travellers. This is the origin of our word, mansion.

MOSAIC A decorative pavement made from small pieces of coloured stone and, occasionally, pieces of glass or pottery. Mosaics may be either "geometric", i.e., composed of linear patterns or motifs; or, "figured" with representations of deities, mythological characters, animals, and so forth. The earliest dated mosaic from Britain comes from the legionary fortress bath house at Exeter (A.D. 55–60) and is closely followed by those in the Fishbourne Roman palace. The great age of mosaics in Britain, however, is the early fourth century A.D.

NOTITIA DIGNITATUM A document usually dated to about A.D. 395 (although only existing today as fifteenth-century and later copies). It is a list of the principal civil and military officials of the empire. Details are given of the stations within each military command and their garrison. It is, therefore, an invaluable document for the study of the late Roman army.

ORCHESTRA In origin this means dance floor and refers to the area between the stage and seating in a theatre.

PALAESTRA Exercise hall of a public bath house where patrons might amuse themselves with games and sports or work up a sweat before bathing.

PARAPET A wall protecting soldiers on the walkway around the top of a fort or town defences.

PEDIMENT A low-pitched gable above classical style porches and doorways such as, for example, the great "gorgon" pediment over the temple entrance at Bath.

PIER Used in architecture to mean a strong solid support for gateways, arches, bridge superstructures, and the like.

PILAE Usually used to refer to pillars supporting the raised floors of hypocaust heating systems. They may be made of stacked tiles or stone blocks.

PLINTH A projecting part of the wall immediately above its base.

PRAEFURNIUM This term meaning "furnace" is usually used in connection with hypocaust systems and bath houses.

PRAETOR A magistrate in Rome. After serving as *praetor*, a man would become eligible for the post of legionary commander.

PRINCIPIA The headquarters building in a fort or fortress consisting of an open courtyard with a cross-hall or basilica on one side.

PROSCAENIUM The Latin word for a theatre stage.

REVETMENT A retaining wall or facing. Early Roman forts in Britain usually had ramparts revetted with stacked turves, material which was obviously in plentiful supply in our temperate climate. When they were made permanent, fort ramparts acquired a stone revetment wall.

SAXON SHORE In Latin, *litus saxonicum*, a term used in the *Notitia Dignitatum* to describe a system of nine forts along the south and east coasts of Britain which together came under the command of the "Count of the Saxon Shore". It is not known when this command came into being, but the system itself was probably the product of gradual development as the forts were founded at different dates. The complete list is Bradwell (Essex), Dover, Lympne, Brancaster (Norfolk), Burgh Castle, Reculver (Kent), Richborough, Pevensey, and a place referred to as Portus Adurni, which may either be Walton (Essex), or Portchester Castle.

SENATOR The highest rank in Roman society. Strictly speaking, to belong to the senatorial class a man needed to own at least one million *sestertii* i.e., there was a wealth qualification, but rank was also passed on by inheritance. As a member of the senatorial class, the way was open to a career in the highest political and military offices. The rank below the senators was known as the "equestrian" order, or knights. They also had certain high-status career opportunities reserved for them.

SIGNIFER A standard bearer. In the Yorkshire Museum, York, there is a well-known tombstone of a standard bearer of the Ninth Legion named Lucius Duccius Rufinus who holds a standard in one hand and a case of writing tablets in the other. The standard bearer who carried the eagle, a legion's most sacred symbol, was known as an *aquilifer*.

TRIBUNAL A raised area for magistrates or military commanders in the basilica of a forum or the cross-hall of a *principia*. The term derives from its association with the tribunes – officers chosen by the people of Rome to protect them against the Senate.

VALLUM Strictly speaking the Latin word *Vallum* refers to an upstanding defensive work, but in a Romano-British context it has come to mean the ditch, with a mound on either side, which ran behind Hadrian's Wall to give the forts along it extra protection.

VICUS (plural *vici*) A term usually used to describe civilian settlements outside forts which may have enjoyed a measure of self-government. Community identity is indicated at Vindolanda by a dedication to Vulcan, patron of metal workers, by the *vicani*, or inhabitants, of the *vicus*.

FURTHER READING

Birley, A. R., *The People of Roman Britain*, Batsford, 1979

Bowman, A. K. & Thomas, J. D., *Vindolanda: The Latin Writing Tablets*, Britannia Monograph Series 4, Society for Promotion of Roman Studies, 1983

Breeze, D. J., & Dobson, B., *Hadrian's Wall*, Penguin, 1976

Carcopino, J., *Daily Life in Ancient Rome*, Penguin, 1956

Collingwood, B. J., *Handbook to the Roman Wall*, ed. and enlargd by C. M. Daniels, Harold Hill, 1978

Crummy, P., *Colchester Archaeological Report 3*, Colchester Archaeological Trust, 1984

Cunliffe, B., *Excavations at Fishbourne 1961–69*, Society of Antiquaries, 1971

Cunliffe, B., & Davenport, P., *The Temple of Sulis Minerva at Bath. Volume I: The Site*, Oxford University Committee for Archaeology, 1986

Detsicas, A., *The Cantiaci*, Alan Sutton, 1983

Frere, S. S., *Britannia*, rev. edn, Routledge & Kegan Paul, 1978

Henig, M., *Religion in Roman Britain*, Batsford, 1984

Johnson, A., *Roman Forts*, A. & C. Black, 1983

Johnson, S., *The Roman Forts of the Saxon Shore*, Elek, 1976

Liversidge, J., *Britain in the Roman Empire*, Routledge & Kegan Paul, 1968

McWhirr, A., Viner, L., and Wells, C., *Romano-British Cemeteries at Cirencester*, Cirencester Excavation Committee, 1982

Marsden, P., *Roman London*, Thames & Hudson, 1980

Milne, G., *The Port of Roman London*, Batsford, 1985

Robertson, A., *The Antonine Wall*, (new edn), Glasgow Archaeological Society, 1979

Royal Commission on Historical Monuments, *The City of York. Volume I: Eburacum*, H.M.S.O., 1962

Salway, P., *Roman Britain*, Oxford University Press, 1981

Wacher, J., *The Towns of Roman Britain*, Batsford, 1974

Webster, G., *The Roman Imperial Army*, A. & C. Black, 1969

Wilson, R. J. A., *A Guide to the Roman Remains in Britain*, 2nd edn, Constable, 1980

Classical Authors

Caesar, *On the Gallic War*, trans. S. A. Handford, Penguin edn

Cassius Dio, *Dio's Roman History*, trans. E. Carey, Loeb Classical Library

Juvenal, *The Sixteen Satires*, trans. P. Green, Penguin edn

Suetonius, *The Twelve Caesars*, trans. R. Graves, Penguin edn

Tacitus, *The Annals of Ancient Rome*, trans. M. Grant, Penguin edn

Tacitus, *The Agricola and The Germania*, trans. H. Mattingly, Penguin edn

Periodicals

News of current work on Roman Britain can be found in:

Britannia, published annually by the society for the Promotion of Roman Studies

British Archaeological News, published monthly by the Council for British Archeology

Current Archaeology, published quarterly

Popular Archaeology, published monthly

Rescue News, published quarterly by Rescue – The British Archaeological Trust

A Note on Roman Names

Roman names, their form, origins and meaning are a very complex subject but travellers may find a few introductory notes of use.

In the first and second centuries A.D. Roman citizens may usually be distinguished because they bear the *tria nomina*, or three names; such as, for example, Gnaeus Julius Agricola. The first name of the three was called the *praenomen*, or forename; the second is the *nomen gentilicium*, equivalent to the modern surname or family name; and the third name is the *cognomen*, a more private or personal name. Until the mid-first century A.D., a cognomen was not universally used and some early tombstones from Britain are of men without one. The problem was, however, that there were relatively few common *praenomina*, so that a *cognomen* became essential to distinguish, to use our previous example, one Gnaeus Julius from another.

Non-citizen Britons usually appear to have been known by only one name, although they were frequently Romanized. When natives became citizens they might integrate their British name into a Roman *tria nomina* by keeping their native name as a *cognomen*. Cogidubnus, for example, styled himself Tiberius Claudius Cogidubnus. He is also one of the first examples in Britain of a person who used the name of the emperor in whose reign he had achieved citizenship. This was to be become a very common practice and, when citizenship was extended to all non-slaves in A.D. 212 by the Emperor Caracalla, his *nomen gentilicium* "Aurelius" became very common in the provinces. Another route to citizenship was as a slave to a citizen and on receiving "manumission" the slave would take the master's *nomen*.

In the third century A.D. conventions changed again as the universal citizenship decree meant that the *tria nomina* no longer had the same significance, and so the *praenomen* virtually disappeared.

The publishers acknowledge with grateful thanks, the help and cooperation of:

Trustees of the Bignor Roman Villa
CADW: Welsh Historical Monuments
English Heritage
National Trust
PJ de Savory, Littecote Limited
Scottish Development Department
Sussex Archaeological Society
Vindolanda Archaeological Trust